Big Nose George

His Troublesome Trail

Big Nose George

His Troublesome Trail

Mark E. Miller

with a foreword by
Lori Van Pelt

HIGH PLAINS PRESS

Library of Congress Cataloging-in-Publication Data

Names: Miller, Mark E., 1951- author.
Title: Big Nose George : his troublesome trail / Mark E. Miller.
Description: Glendo, WY : High Plains Press, [2021] | Includes bibliographical references and index. | Summary: "The biography of "Big Nose George" Parott who was involved in the murder of two lawmen in Carbon County Wyoming and died in a lynching in 1881. In the aftermath, his skullcap was preserved and his skin made into a pair of shoes"-- Provided by publisher.
Identifiers: LCCN 2021016828 (print) | LCCN 2021016829 (ebook) | ISBN 9781937147266 (hardcover) | 9781937147242 (trade paperback) | ISBN 9781937147259 (kindle edition)
Subjects: LCSH: Parrott, Big Nose George, -1881 | Outlaws--West (U.S.)--Biography. | Crime--West (U.S.) | Frontier and pioneer life--West (U.S.)--Biography.
Classification: LCC F594.P37 M55 2021 (print) | LCC F594.P37 (ebook) | DDC 364.152/3092 [B]--dc23
LC record available at https://lccn.loc.gov/2021016828
LC ebook record available at https://lccn.loc.gov/2021016829

FIRST PRINTING
10 9 8 7 6 5 4 3 2 1
Manufactured in the United States of America

HIGH PLAINS PRESS
403 CASSA ROAD, GLENDO, WY 82213
WWW.HIGHPLAINSPRESS.COM
ORDERS & CATALOGS: 1-800-552-7819

Dedicated to the memory of

Robert Widdowfield and

Henry H. "Tip" Vincent

"This is the West, sir.

When the legend becomes fact, print the legend."

—from the screenplay

The Man Who Shot Liberty Valance

Contents

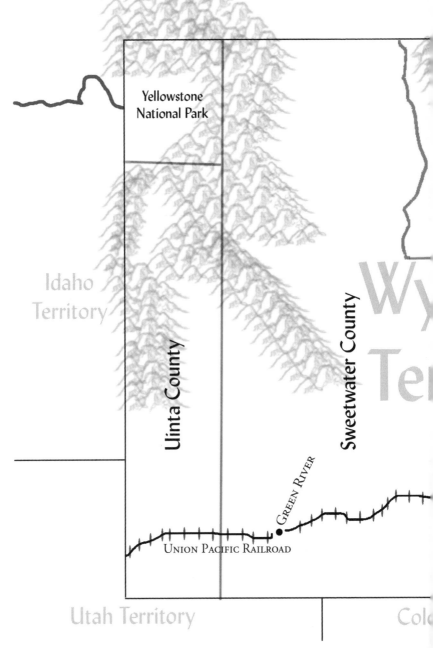

Big Nose George's \

Yellowstone
National Park

Idaho
Territory

Uinta County

Sweetwater County

W

Te

GREEN RIVER

UNION PACIFIC RAILROAD

Utah Territory

Col

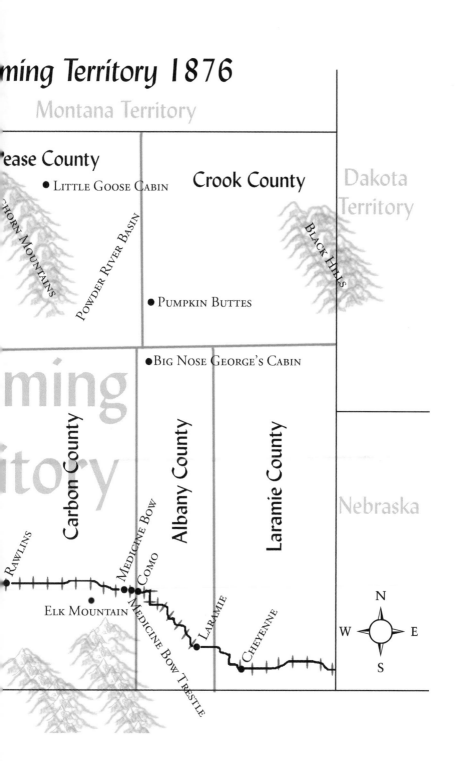

ming Territory 1876

Montana Territory

'ease County
● LITTLE GOOSE CABIN

Crook County

Dakota
Territory

CHORN MOUNTAINS

POWDER RIVER BASIN

BLACK HILLS

● PUMPKIN BUTTES

ming

itory

●BIG NOSE GEORGE'S CABIN

Carbon County

Albany County

Laramie County

Nebraska

MEDICINE BOW

COMO

● RAWLINS

LARAMIE

CHEYENNE

ELK MOUNTAIN
●

MEDICINE BOW TRESTLE

N
W ✦ E
S

Foreword

THE STORY OF Big Nose George Parott includes many of the elements that create long-lasting Old West legends: an attempted train robbery, murder, an attempted jailbreak, and vigilante justice. This particular tale has intrigued people and fascinated historians for more than 140 years and quite often is told with a slant toward the more grotesque and haunting aspects. Some could probably pass off the more bizarre pieces as simply imagination run wild. For example, did a doctor who became a Wyoming governor actually wear shoes made from the tanned hide of the outlaw to his inauguration? But evidence exists: court transcripts, coroner's inquests, the skull, a death mask,—and, of course, the shoes.

In the midst of all of the sensational details, the graves of the two lawmen killed in the line of duty—and the significance of their work and their lives—sometimes recedes to the background.

In this book, Dr. Mark Miller, the great-grandson of Isaac C. "Ike" Miller, who served as Carbon County Sheriff when Parott was jailed in Rawlins, draws upon the family stories he heard as a youth about the events of that earlier era and incorporates his scientific experience as a former Wyoming State Archaeologist to create a thorough and compelling study of the criminal activities of Big Nose George Parott in the years 1876–1881. He brings the Carbon County events into clearer focus by following the facts while broadening the picture to include other activities that were important in the area and the nation at the time, such as dinosaur fossil explorations.

Miller searched through court and museum records, studied artifacts held in museum and archival collections, and sifted through the work of previous historians and articles in the *Carbon County*

Journal and other newspapers. He conducted field studies at the sites of the attempted train robbery, at the ghost town of Carbon, and at the murder scene. Maps created by the Wyoming State Historic Preservation Office and the author enable readers to better visualize the locations. In addition, Miller includes details from Dr. George Gill's biological and forensic work in 1995 on the skull and offers suggestions about whether using modern DNA analysis could resolve lingering questions about Parott's heritage and match him with possible family members.

Reflecting upon the rippling effect that the historic events have upon current and future generations—not least among them the importance of the deputies who were killed—Miller poses some weighty questions:

"How then does a community's sense of justice reflect in its social character after nearly a century and a half have passed? Should myths take precedence over historical facts? Will truth about the whole Parott affair ever overshadow his colorful legend? These questions permeate the social character of Rawlins today as it comes to grips with how to portray the Elk Mountain affair as a crucial episode in its local history."

Miller's engaging and well-balanced narrative tells the story of Big Nose George Parott in a straightforward manner that speaks to the legend and clarifies the historical record. This impressive work will no doubt become a "go-to" source for historians and readers for generations to come.

—LORI VAN PELT
Laramie, WY

Preface

THE EPIGRAPH introducing this book reflects the imprecise nature of territorial news coverage typical of the nineteenth-century American West. It reads: "This is the West, Sir. When the legend becomes fact, print the legend."

The quote comes from dialogue near the end of the movie, *The Man Who Shot Liberty Valance,* directed by John Ford and released in 1962. In that film, the legend refers to an event widely believed to be true and retold by the townspeople of Shinbone, but found to be false at the end of the story.

There is veracity to this quote for some people who ponder the West, but it misleads those searching for truth. Legends too often overshadow facts as they grow in media popularity, especially when the criminal activity of Big Nose George 140 years ago is considered.

It seems fitting for me to write this brief history of nineteenth-century outlaw Big Nose George Parott, whose criminal exploits spanned 1876–1881 in Wyoming Territory. After all, four generations of Millers grew up telling his story because parts of it hit close to home. My great-grandfather, Isaac C. (Ike) Miller, was Carbon County Sheriff when a Powder River Gang member sat in jail after his turbulent criminal trial in Rawlins. Sheriff Miller was legally required to carry out the sentence imposed by the court on the prisoner.

I was born in that railroad town seventy years after Parott's death. Every kid my age grew up wide-eyed, hearing similar harrowing accounts of the Elk Mountain incident and the outlaw gang who perpetrated it. Most out-of-town visitors to Rawlins heard it as well. In fact, the event is still, at this writing, prominently featured in our community at the county museum and on a large billboard near the railroad depot.

Scores of news articles, books, internet sources, and pamphlets relate the traumatic incidents of Parott's later life. While his saga fascinates a wide and diverse audience, the factual story itself is more difficult to tell. Two of the most accurate and comprehensive treatments of Big Nose George were written by noted historians Daniel Y. Meschter[1] and Max Atwell,[2] but both of these sources were privately published and not widely circulated.

Parott's exploits as a notorious desperado are only one example of extreme violence perpetrated in Wyoming during the late nineteenth century. Popular accounts portray other crimes as well, such as the lynching of Ella Watson (Cattle Kate) and James Averell in 1889 and the Johnson County Cattle War of 1892. The more often these stories are told, and the more people who tell them, the greater they grow in bravado and exaggeration. Western legends are born this way.

Many authors have frequently repeated brief snippets of Parott's chaotic life from so many different perspectives that his final years have evolved into one of these classic western legends. Exposing his true saga is fraught with confusing historical statements and sparse eyewitness detail. Even so, any author writing about the man must refer to these often-ambiguous accounts because they constitute much of the written record of his legacy.

Wickedness, like all forms of human behavior, is a remarkably complex subject to comprehend, so we depend on as many sources of evidence as possible to help illuminate the nature of criminal deeds. Yet, while eyewitnesses may write about actual events first-hand, their real time advantage does not always yield a clear picture of the cultural matrix of current events. Eye-catching headlines typically carried the day in newspapers of the nineteenth century, while factual accounts of western outlaws were seldom covered in adequate detail. Modern researchers therefore need more than the written record to build a comprehensive picture of the subject.

Objective research on such topics requires critical assessment. Since it is human nature to err at times while recording perceived truths, legends become comingled with facts during the recounting of distant exploits. Truths and falsehoods are stirred into a cauldron of tainted literary brew. Big Nose George's life story suffers from this flaw, so scientific investigations have been added to the analysis of his corrupt life.

Archaeological research and forensic study are included here to expand our interpretive potential beyond the written historical record. Archaeology is the scientific study of human behavior that examines physical evidence left behind in artifacts and sites after an event occurs. Forensics are scientific techniques used in the investigation of a crime, in this instance of a very cold murder case.

Artifact patterning enables valuable interpretations of past activities, but noted archeologist Lewis Binford warns analysts to develop explanatory models of human activity rather than attempt to fully explain past behavior. His cautionary note is necessary, because we cannot really acquire "a direct knowledge of the essential properties of the world."[3] We can never "prove" details of past behavior.

Our explanatory models come from specific frames of reference we establish when looking at human behavior. Formation processes in the archaeological record, for example, allow us to give greater meaning to artifact patterns as they relate to past conduct. Kristina McMahan, a graduate student at the time, noted this multidisciplinary approach when she advocated integration of period documents with current anthropological research to develop a more complete understanding of Parott's final years.[4] History, archaeology, and forensic research serve as compatible tools for describing George Parott's criminal activity between 1876 and 1881.

Parott's final years in Wyoming Territory produced savage events that led to his ultimate death more than two years after the August 19, 1878, Elk Mountain incident. Hopefully, the behavioral model presented here accurately reflects Parott's criminal life and the events that followed his death. While gaps in our knowledge still exist, many others were filled in with inferential arguments that present the reader with a more complete flow of probable actions. Future research undoubtedly will expand our discovery of new facts, taking us closer toward truth and further from legend.

—MARK E. MILLER

Big Nose George's portrait photograph is believed to have been taken in Omaha, 1880. *Courtesy, Carbon County Museum, Rawlins, Wyoming.*

Cast of Characters

WHAT FOLLOWS IS a brief description of many of the individuals in the book, listed alphabetically in three categories. The spelling for the names used throughout this book is in bold face. Spelling alternatives and some aliases follow the names.

Dr. David Throgmorton, a Rawlins educator, prepared a typed, unpublished manuscript on the Big Nose George story and its relevance to the sense of entitlement exhibited by wealthy and connected individuals in the mythic West.[1] Much of his source material comes from handwritten documents he researched in the Montana State Historical Society Archives in Helena, which includes written descriptions provided by Sheriff Irvine in March 1880 of several of the outlaws listed. Genealogist Sandra Jones shared the brief physical description of Robert Widdowfield.

— *Outlaws* —

Jack Campbell. An outlaw in Montana and Wyoming who rode for an extended period with Big Nose George Parott in the Powder River Gang. He was about five feet, ten inches tall, 135–140 pounds, with sandy hair, long red whiskers, and dark eyes. He had a squeaky voice and constantly coughed, but he was described as a gentleman. This enigmatic individual escaped justice for his role in the ruthless Wyoming crime spree.

Dutch Charley (Burris, Bates, Clark, Randall, One-Winged Charley). Another one of eight Powder River badmen who rode in the gang with Big Nose George into Carbon County, Wyoming. He may have been a cavalry deserter involved in horse stealing and other crimes in the Powder River and Black Hills area. He died at the hands of an irate lynch mob in the coal town of Carbon in January 1879.

Frank James (McKinney). Older of the two famous outlaw brothers, Frank and Jesse, who committed crimes in Missouri and elsewhere after the Civil War. He and Big Nose George organized the eight-member Powder River Gang that rode into Carbon County intending to wreak havoc. McKinney was described as tall with square shoulders, polite, and sporting reddish whiskers that he constantly picked at. His identity as one of the famous James Brothers is often debated by historians.

Joe Minuse (John Minuse, Manuse). An outlaw who suffered through a murder trial in Rawlins, but was found not guilty. He never rode with the Powder River Gang, but later served time in Laramie for other unrelated offenses.

Big Nose George Parott (Parrot, Parrott, Bill Dixon, George Reynolds, George Francis Warden). George worked for a time as a mule skinner for the Central Pacific Railroad in Utah before turning to a life of crime. He helped Frank James organize the Powder River Gang in August 1878 for a rendezvous with destiny in Carbon County, Wyoming.

Tom Reed (Tim Reed). Reed was five feet, five inches tall, weighed 145 pounds, had dark hair and stubby whiskers. He wore a gold ring on the third finger of his left hand and was about thirty years old. Reed also escaped punishment for his complicity in the Carbon County affair and was never arrested for the crimes.

Frank Tole (Frank Towle). A former laborer for J. Elmer Brock in the Powder River Basin, Tole often terrorized stage shipments on the Black Hills line. He was the first of the Powder River Gang to die following a bloody encounter in Carbon County.

Sim Wan (Wann). Another one of the eight members of the Powder River Gang. His own identity often was confused with other men, including Jesse James for a time. He was shorter than Campbell, with light colored hair and whiskers and blue eyes. He was twenty-six years old at the time of the crime and was never caught.

John Wells (Sandy). Wells was about five feet, seven inches tall, 140 pounds, with short stubby hair and red whiskers. He was quiet and surly. This eighth gang member skipped justice completely it seems, and disappeared into the annals of western history. He may have been the most elusive outlaw of them all.

— *Lawmen* —

M.F. Leech. Leech was a former Union Pacific Railroad detective who maintained a keen interest in solving the 1878 crimes in Carbon County perpetrated by the Powder River Gang. He pulled off a real prosecutorial coup by getting one of the gang members to retell the entire story of their criminal spree following the man's arrest, thus sealing the outlaw's fate.

Isaac C. "Ike" Miller. A prominent stockman and civic leader who beat Rankin in the 1880 sheriff's election. Miller took office as one gang member's trial ended and his incarceration continued. Miller was charged by statute to carry out the legal requirements imposed by the man's sentence.

James Rankin. The undersheriff for Ike Lawry led an August 18, 1878, chase after the Powder River Gang once they retreated from an aborted robbery attempt near Como Bluff. Rankin ran for Carbon County Sheriff in 1880 shortly after he brought one of the perpetrators back to Rawlins for trial, but was defeated in the election by Miller.

Henry H. "Tip" Vincent (Vinson, Vincents). A popular Carbon County man hired as a detective by the Union Pacific Railroad to track down the Powder River Gang after their attempted robbery. He was well known in the area and quite familiar with the Como Bluff region.

Robert Widdowfield. He was deputy sheriff under Ike Lawry and worked out of the coal town of Carbon. He also tracked the Powder River Gang with Vincent after the outlaws escaped toward Elk Mountain. He was a stocky man with blond hair and had a family in Carbon.

— Other Important Characters —

William E. Carlin. Hired by Professor Othniel Marsh of Yale University to collect dinosaur fossils with William H. Reed in the Como Bluff quarries around the time the Powder River Gang arrived. He identified the recent crime scene to another paleontologist, Arthur Lakes, who chronicled the site location in his journal.

Lillian Heath. Lillian Heath was a teenager when her family came to Rawlins, Wyoming, where she soon began assisting Dr. Thomas Maghee in his medical practice. She became the first woman physician in Wyoming and kept an object given to her by Maghee's partner in 1881 that helped solve an outlaw's identity seventy years later.

John Osborne. A medical doctor who came to Rawlins to practice with local doctor Maghee while one of the Powder River Gang members was incarcerated. Osborne eventually became Wyoming Governor, a U.S. Congressman, and Under Secretary of State in the Wilson administration.

Chapter One

A Sinister Cloud Gathers

Two horses stomped the firm ground, cutting through bent grass around the smoldering campfire. The tallest rider dismounted, walked over to feel heat from the fire's embers, and said something to his partner on horseback. Suddenly, the sound of a rifle shot rang through the mountain air. A large caliber lead bullet ripped through the aspen leaves into the clearing, struck the standing man in his eye, and blew away half of his face. He dropped dead on top of the warm coals.

His partner galloped away only to be knocked out of his saddle by a powerful gunshot in the back. This second man died while pointing his revolver toward a group of surly gunmen who had moved out of their forested concealment near the fire. Afterward, Rattlesnake Canyon quieted down once more as the soft breeze fluttered through the leaves dangling from a thousand aspen branches. These grisly murders produced the apex moment in the early history of Carbon County, Wyoming, and helped define the social character of Rawlins for over a century.

BIG NOSE GEORGE PAROTT participated in this and other crimes throughout Montana and Wyoming during his callous and tragic life as a western outlaw, a life that brutally terminated in Rawlins, Wyoming, on March 22, 1881. We first hear of him as a Montana horse thief living under the alias of George Reynolds.

In 1948, author Bennett Stein[1] found a lengthy manuscript written by Montana pioneer, Andrew Garcia, that had been stored for decades in some dynamite boxes. Garcia had written his memories down when he was over sixty, after years spent wandering the Montana wilderness with some of the most dubious associates possible. His memoir included firsthand observations of an outlaw with a large nose who eventually became a legend in Wyoming Territory.

On one trip in early to mid-July 1878, Garcia started off on horseback from Fort Ellis near Bozeman with a sidekick named Beaver Tom to hunt and trap the country around the Musselshell River. Beaver Tom typically drank too much so Garcia did most of the work, but both were out for pure adventure, and they seem to have found it. The two men soon encountered three unsavory characters going in the same direction, and they all rode together on the trip. One of the heavily armed desperados was called George Reynolds, who later proved to be Big Nose George Parott. He had ridden up from Utah via Green River, Wyoming, accompanied by his partner, Al Shinnick.[2]

Parott was about thirty-five years old in 1878. He had been an outlaw for several years, beginning in Utah after finishing his employment as a teamster on the Central Pacific Railroad and continuing through episodes of horse stealing and stage robbery in the intermountain West. He also may have once had honest work as a bull team driver on the Black Hills freight route for a time,[3] which would have given him good opportunity to scout that area for potential holdup locations.

Before getting to Montana, Parott and Shinnick had wanted to rob the Utah-Montana stages but found they were too well protected so they aborted their plans.[4] When the two men did head to Montana, they may have passed through Powder River country and stopped for a rest at a place where Parott established a cabin/dugout on Sand Creek south of Pumpkin Buttes in Wyoming. It would be a good spot to recuperate between jobs.

Garcia and his mixed group of trappers and thieves continued on the trail together for several days, passing the Shields River, Big Timber, and the Sweet Grass on their way to the Musselshell. He grew more and more wary of his uninvited guests, who later were joined by a couple more riders farther out on the trail. The group of outsiders gave whiskey to the Indians in exchange for horses throughout the trip and eventually trailed a growing herd of over one hundred animals toward the Musselshell country while riding alongside the trappers.

One of the new arrivals partnered with Reynolds (Parott) to trade one quart of whiskey to the Crows for each one of their horses, but they did not trade for mares. Mares could be a problem in a mixed herd and slow down travel especially if the animals were pregnant. This newly arrived horse thief told Garcia they were headed toward Canada to sell the entire herd to the Mounties. But the man quickly took a powerful dislike to Garcia, not trusting him to keep quiet about their scheme, and was planning to kill him once they made their next camp.

Events came to a head near Judith Gap north of the Musselshell River where three of the thieves, including Reynolds (Parott), convinced Garcia to leave the party before any blood was shed. In their own way, they were trying to keep Garcia alive. After Garcia and Beaver Tom left the group, the thieves continued on toward the Canadian border another 165 miles away, arriving there about July 23, 1878, where they sold the horse herd. They certainly would have traveled faster after the trappers left with their loaded pack horses.

Historians know that Big Nose George Parott participated in criminal activity near Medicine Bow in Carbon County, Wyoming less than a month later, on August 17, 1878. Medicine Bow is about five hundred miles south of the Canadian border. If Big Nose George left Canada on horseback July 23, he had around twenty-five days to reach Medicine Bow, covering about twenty miles per day. This would be a relatively easy feat for a practiced rider with a good mount, so he may have ridden closer to thirty-five miles per day since he had something to do in Wyoming.

Big Nose George's plan in Carbon County required the assistance of several partners, so he needed to put together a Powder River outlaw gang once he returned to Wyoming. The first prominent gang member would be Frank James, arguably the older brother of the famous outlaw Jesse James. Frank was hiding out in northern

This portrait shows Frank James, brother of Jesse James, in 1898. *Courtesy, Library of Congress, Prints and Photographs Division, LC-USZ62-38208.*

Wyoming at the time, although healthy debate exists regarding his whereabouts between July 1878 and April 1879.

Outlaw gangs of the late nineteenth-century American West were a fluid and dynamic mix of miscreants and evildoers, never staying together very long, and certainly not holding powerful allegiances among group members. An outlaw may have been in one man's gang for a heist, then moved on to another gang for a separate caper, offering little or no explanation for his maneuver. This blending of gangs, combined with the ubiquitous use of aliases and obscure personal identity traits, makes detailed research of their exploits a difficult proposition indeed. Such ephemeral outlaw gangs had become the scourge of eastern Montana and Wyoming in the late 1870s, and the growing Powder River Gang of 1878 was a good example.

Frank was a logical choice to be a leading gang member. In September 1876, the James and Younger brothers had attempted a bank robbery in Northfield, Minnesota, but were badly beaten back by armed residents in the community. Lawmen chased the retreating outlaws away from town. A sheriff's posse flushed the gang out of the thick woods fifteen miles west of Northfield shortly afterward. The gang split up a few days later, riding through the Blue Earth Woods and heading for Mankato in southern Minnesota. Jesse and Frank made it into Dakota Territory, but their trail vanished at Sioux Falls. Frank may have entered Wyoming for a time soon thereafter.

Little is actually known about the James Brothers' whereabouts from September 1876 to October 1879. The two men were in and out of Missouri a bit, but they traveled about for a few years as well. The Powder River country was wide open at the time, and quite suitable for two men wanting to lay low out of sight of the law. It is possible one or both James boys entered Wyoming Territory in the fall of 1876, but Frank certainly seems to have done so by the spring of 1878.[5] They established a hideout cabin along Little Goose Creek at that time, near the present-day community of Big Horn, Wyoming.

Frank eventually traveled to Nashville, Tennessee, with his wife and son to take up a successful effort at farming during part of this three-year hiatus.[6] Both he and Jesse were living under aliases, and if they spent some of their time in Wyoming, they must have traveled back and forth to Tennessee where their families were in hiding.[7] This mobility would have been a simple procedure, made easy by riding the railroads under aliases and disguise.

According to local families, the James brothers periodically stayed at their hideout along a secluded segment of the Little Goose Valley north of the new Fort McKinney, Wyoming. They occupied a two-room cabin with a barn and stables large enough to hold twenty horses.[8] A Black cook named John took care of the hideout and served the James brothers when they lived there.

Other interpretations of the brothers' whereabouts have been published elsewhere. For instance, James biographer Breihan acknowledges Frank's role in the Powder River Gang and the cabin near Big Horn, and also describes the brothers travelling through Texas and Mexico during the same time.[9] Discrepancy between these two theories may one day be resolved if more evidence comes to light.

Regardless, a man named Frank James figures prominently in primary documents related to the present story, and evidence from early local residents argues that the famous James brother was indeed in Wyoming.[10] Frank was about thirty-five years old in 1878 and had proven to be an accomplished train robber. He and his brother Jesse had terrorized communities from Missouri to Minnesota since 1868. While Frank's time in Wyoming between 1876 and 1879 was disrupted on occasion by further criminal acts, visits to family in Tennessee, and the threat of Indian fights, he avoided serious confrontations with the law while ensconced in his hideout.

Frank's Little Goose Creek hideout was Big Nose George's destination when he traveled the first three-hundred-mile leg of his journey from Canada to northern Wyoming. By riding thirty-five miles per day and allowing for reasonable breaks, Parott could have been at the cabin in about nine days, arriving sometime around August 1. Frank James was there, but Jesse was away.

———

Little Goose Creek flows into a tributary of Powder River where it bisects a vast, high plains grassland basin. Powder River country spans the distance between the North Platte River valley to the south and the Yellowstone River valley to the north. The towering Big Horn Mountains flank its western boundary, and headwaters of east flowing drainages carve a hydrographic divide between the Black Hills region along the South Dakota border and the Powder River drainage.

Powder River country is highlighted by Pumpkin Buttes in the background. This contemporary photo shows South, South Middle, Indian, and North Middle Buttes. *Mark Fisher Photograph (wyogeo.com).*

The area had been home to vast herds of bison (buffalo), and the nomadic horse culture of American Indian tribes in precontact times. Euroamerican settlers then began to occupy the region in the 1860s; the U.S. Army removed Indians from the Powder River Basin a decade or so later. This demographic shift opened the vast region to immigrant entrepreneurs in search of their own fortunes.

Once word got out that prospectors had discovered gold in 1862 Montana, federal authorities sought to construct a transportation route to deliver goods, services, and people from the well-traveled Oregon Trail in southern Wyoming, across Powder River country, to the new Montana gold fields.[11] Relations between Indian nations and the U.S. Government there had been relatively calm until development of this Bozeman Trail, which strained peaceful negotiations. The growing influx of travelers on the Bozeman increased difficulties until armed conflicts erupted into the Indian War of 1865–1868.[12]

Tensions mellowed for a few years after 1868, until the discovery of Black Hills gold in 1874 reignited problems. By then the U.S. Army had established a network of forts along the Union Pacific in the south and the Missouri River in the north and east, effectively surrounding the Sioux and Northern Cheyenne in the Powder River country with some five thousand garrisoned soldiers along a twenty-five-hundred-mile perimeter.[13]

The presence of garrisoned troops was soon followed by ranching operations and fledgling settlements along major drainages, and these locations held a supply of horses, frequent gold shipments, and growing citizen wealth. The basin became a target-rich environment for outlaws more willing to steal from others than work honestly for their own riches.

As gold seekers flocked into the Black Hills, military garrisons had to protect settlers and mining interests as they spilled over into Indian territory. The growing Euroamerican presence in the Black Hills eventually prompted final removal of free roaming Indian populations from the Powder River country a couple of short years later.

Ironically, the attendant violence that followed the expanding outlaw presence in Powder River country occurred just as the region was being pacified by the removal of hostile Indians. Outlaws living there could now go almost unchallenged after horses, gold, and other loot clear to the railroad in the south, the Black Hills in the east, and the Yellowstone River in the north. Loosely organized gangs of desperados began conducting all sorts of nefarious activities.

—•—

After Parott's arrival at the Little Goose Creek hideout, he probably secured a fresh mount, and spent a few days with Frank James planning their joint caper. The two outlaws had a couple of weeks to develop and finalize tactics for a train derailment and robbery along the UPRR in southern Wyoming, to organize and connect with the rest of what became their Powder River Gang, and still get to Medicine Bow by August 17. Parott and James had plenty of time to ride the remaining 230-mile distance to the railroad, even allowing for time to hook up with dispersed gang members coming from various points in the Powder River country. Parott's cabin and dugout south of Pumpkin Buttes was the probable rendezvous point for members of the group.

The location of Big Nose George's cabin is identified on Holt's 1883 map of Wyoming, compiled in 1882 only a year after the outlaw's death.[14] It sits near the Fort Caspar and Powder River Road, adjacent to Sand Creek, a tributary in the Cheyenne River drainage about thirty-six miles south of Pumpkin Buttes. His cabin is strategically situated only a few miles west of the Fort Fetterman to Fort McKinney stage road that follows some of the old Bozeman Trail route.

A man named Mermardi, deputy surveyor in this area for the General Land Office (GLO), shows the cabin to be in the northwest quarter of Section 34, in Township 39 North, Range 75 West.[15] Not surprisingly, no official records of land transactions appear for the township any time before 1897. Parott had not filed on a land claim and might not have wanted the location advertised publicly.

This remote hideout was ideal for outlaws traveling southeast from Little Goose Creek to meet up with outlaws traveling southwest from the Deadwood stage line in the Black Hills. Cabin occupants could see any intruders approach, allowing quick escape in any direction if threatened by outside forces.

—•—

What stimulus might compel a group of outlaws to ride over two hundred miles from northern Wyoming to the UPRR for a robbery? Knowledge of an early 1878 event may answer this question. In that incident, four masked men boarded the westbound Number Three passenger train just as it left Percy Station in Carbon County about 10:00 P.M. on Wednesday, May 29, 1878. Several robbers walked into the second sleeper car wearing masks, held guns on the occupants, forced them to raise their hands, and then proceeded to remove any personal valuables from the startled travelers.[16]

The bandits didn't manage to gather a significant amount of loot in the five minutes they were there, perhaps only a few hundred dollars' worth of trinkets. Then they stopped the train to disembark and ran away toward the north. Fifteen men from Rawlins and elsewhere mounted up at eight the next morning and started tracking the trail of the outlaws. Joe Adams, a railroad employee from Rawlins, and deputies representing Carbon County Sheriff Ike

Lawry rode in the posse and were soon met by soldiers from Fort Steele. Additional men came from Carbon to help, including the deputy sheriff there.

The retreating outlaws left on foot toward the Medicine Bow River, eventually boarded a raft they had hidden in the brush, and escaped down the North Platte through the river canyon cut into the Seminoe Mountains. Unfortunately, their raft broke up against the rocks jutting out in the rapids, and they were quickly captured on shore by the posse.[17]

This train robbery in Carbon County became a major story, even though the nearest newspaper was at Laramie in Albany County to the east. The *Laramie Daily Sentinel* printed an extensive account of the Percy robbery in its Thursday, May 30, 1878, issue, complete with many details either known or suspected at the time. For some unfathomable reason, the article declared, "no one thought the train from the east would be attacked, as it was the one from the west which carries the treasure, and which it was of course expected the suspicious men would attempt to rob."[18] Any literate outlaw who read a copy of this paper would learn exactly which train to target during a future heist. The media had revealed sensitive information unnecessarily, and outlaws on Little Goose Creek eventually took advantage of it.

Specific knowledge of a treasure train on the UPRR may have provided the motive to pull together the Powder River Gang before the Medicine Bow incident in August 1878. Planning a successful heist of the Number Four eastbound treasure train would require the cooperation of several outlaws, experienced leadership regarding train derailments, good horses, and a failsafe escape plan. Consequently, Frank James and Big Nose George had begun gathering experienced help by contacting some of their compadres in the Powder River and Black Hills regions.

Some of their gang members even left honest employment for a criminal career and eventually joined the outlaw band. One of these was Frank Tole who had worked for Elmer Brock near the first site of Fort McKinney, a military installation on the Powder River in

1878 before it was moved to a new site near Buffalo, Wyoming. Well-known Powder River rancher J. Elmer Brock had secured beef and woodcutting contracts to supply troops at the fort when it was still located along the Powder River. In the spring of 1878, two unnamed men rode into the wood camp to talk with one of his woodcutters, an employee named Frank Tole.[19]

Tole had just finished cutting four hundred cords of wood at two dollars per cord when the riders arrived. The two strangers seemed well acquainted with Tole, and they came back the next day for further discussion with him. After that second parlay, Tole told his employer he would be leaving his woodcutting job and gathered his pay of eight hundred dollars. Brock was suspicious of the two visitors, but had to let Tole leave with them.

These two men were likely Frank Howard and Dutch Charley, the latter of whom apparently had spent time recently around Sidney, Nebraska. Howard later admitted to authorities he first met Dutch Charley in February 1878 in the Powder River country and rode with him for three months or more. Dutch Charley was recovering from a gunshot wound in the arm at the time, hence his nickname One-Winged Charley. He was looking for work that spring and already was known to be a notorious horse thief.[20]

Frank Tole and his two compadres, Howard and Dutch Charley, left the wood camp, turned back after riding just a short distance, and proceeded to rob Brock of several horses and equipment, trailing the animals toward Deadwood. Such criminal behavior was a typical trait of Tole's. Only a year earlier, he had been implicated as an accomplice in the April 4, 1877, robbery of the Cheyenne and Black Hills stage line where a stage driver was murdered.[21]

Tole proved to be familiar with the stage line through the Black Hills, the valuables it carried, and the act of homicide. On July 25, 1878, he participated in a gang that attempted robbery of the mail stage on the Deadwood line. Tole's new gang consisted of himself and five partners. Three of these outlaws were Jack Campbell, Tom Reed, and a deserter from the Third Cavalry[22] who may have been Tole's pal Dutch Charley. We know from later evidence that Dutch

Charley owned a Springfield Breechloading carbine, which would have been military issue.

The mail stage gang split up after the robbery attempt. Frank Tole, Jack Campbell, Tom Reed, and Dutch Charley apparently continued riding into the Powder River Basin toward Big Nose George's cabin south of Pumpkin Buttes to rest up and join the growing Powder River Gang. They must have received word earlier from James and Parott about plans to put together the gang. The cabin was an ideal spot to meet the two men coming down from Little Goose Creek.

This collective scenario accounts for all but two of the gang that entered Carbon County with criminal intent on August 17, 1878. Sim Wan and John Wells (Sandy) must have joined the six others about this time as well. Historians seem to know less about these two outlaws than any of the others in the gang. Perhaps Big Nose George picked them up somewhere in the Powder River Basin, or they may have been at the Little Goose Creek cabin when Parott arrived from his Canadian sojourn. At any rate, the eight riders were now a single unit and they prepared to leave the Powder River country together, heading south toward the UPRR between Medicine Bow and Como Bluff.

Once the gang left Parott's cabin on their way to the railroad, they still had to travel over one hundred miles to arrive on the evening of August 16, 1878. They left the cabin about August 13, which would allow for an easy ride and also give the gang plenty of time to work out final details of the railroad heist.

Frank James, Big Nose George Parott, Dutch Charley, Frank Tole, Jack Campbell, Tom Reed, Sim Wan, and John Wells spurred their horses along the dusty trail leading southwest over the drainage divide from the Powder River Basin into the North Platte valley, rode across the river, and passed the eastern foot of the Freezeout Mountains.

The sprawling country of northern Carbon County was not too difficult for them to travel. The North Platte River valley opened into low, rolling hills in the Shirley Basin that continued on south to the gradual grade of the Union Pacific Railroad, which connected the east and west coasts of America for thousands of travelers. The rugged Rocky Mountains loomed thirty-five miles to the south and were first distinguished by the prominent slopes of Elk Mountain jutting out into the high plains.

The determined band of outlaws from Powder River country probably rode at night to avoid being seen by local residents. They had a covert mission to perform. Their clandestine trail eventually led the eight men to the western edge of Como Bluff, to infamy, and into the darkest pages of American history.

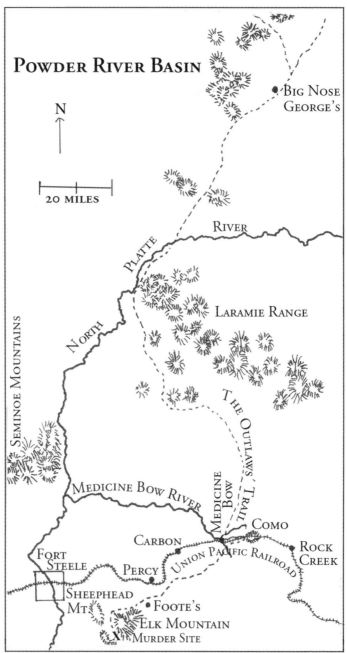

This map shows the James/Parott outlaw trail, Powder River Basin to Elk Mountain. *Adapted from GLO maps by author.*

Chapter Two

A Failed Robbery and Cold-Blooded Murder

THE POWDER RIVER GANG rode down the hillslope into the Medicine Bow River valley and saw the few lights twinkling in the distance at the railroad station and small community of Medicine Bow. Como Bluff rose above the valley just a few miles east of the town along the railroad track. The bluff area had become popular the year before as a dinosaur hunting paradise for paleontologists to collect fossils from the many outcrops adjacent to the railroad. It was Friday evening, August 16, when the gang crept into town in search of a tool shed near the railroad tracks where they could equip themselves for the planned heist.

Once they found the shed, the outlaws broke in, stole a sledge hammer and other implements, intending to draw out railroad spikes and remove fish plates to ditch the train somewhere down the line away from town. Fish plates were the metal bars bolted across the ends of adjoining rails that connected them into a single track. Once the plates were taken away, the outlaws could pull up spikes and move the rails out of alignment.

Parott and the others gathered the tools they needed, then bedded down in the nearby hills until the next morning. Once awake, they rode eastward on Saturday morning, August 17, and stopped where the railroad tracks cross a narrow, wooden trestle that spanned a shallow ravine off the western end of Como Bluff. They were about five miles out of Medicine Bow. Each man went to work to sabotage the tracks in preparation for the upcoming "treasure train."

Como Bluff in 1878 was well known nationwide for its many exposed bedrock formations containing rich hordes of dinosaur fossils. The area was considered "one of the greatest assemblages of giant and small dinosaurs and of minute and extremely precious Jurassic mammals ever to be found."[1] Yale's Peabody Museum had collected fossils there since 1877 and shipped them on the UPRR to their laboratories back east. Como, the first railroad station east of Medicine Bow, served as the shipping point for the fossils. The station was about a mile east of the wooden trestle and hidden from view by the nose of Como Bluff.

Fossil collectors, William Reed and William Carlin, who once had been railroad men themselves, were doing much of the actual collecting. They hired an assistant named Vincent in late 1877 to help them hunt the area and gather dinosaur specimens for the Peabody Museum. Unfortunately, Vincent's first name is not given in their accounts, so we don't know his exact identity.

Fossil collecting was rigorous and demanding. Vincent and his friends must have gotten in great shape during their stay. At one distant fossil locality on the eastern end of the bedrock outcrops, the team had to encase several large bones in plaster casts for protection during transport. Then they hand-carried these heavy specimens across a nearby creek to the edge of the railroad tracks. From that point, the collecting crew used a railroad handcar to move the finds west to Como Station.[2] The men's connection with the railroad helped them get permission to use a cart for transportation. This arduous labor continued until the end of August 1878 when collecting stopped.

In spite of obtaining the UPRR car, the three men suffered from a frustrating lack of support from their sponsor throughout 1877–1878, and they encountered trouble during a dispute with Yale representative Professor Othniel Marsh over back wages owed to each of them. These mounting difficulties precipitated Vincent's resignation as a fossil collector in late March 1878,[3] but he may have stuck around the area seeking new employment with the railroad.

The fossil collector Vincent may be the same man as thirty-nine-year-old Henry H. "Tip" Vincent who figures prominently in the this book. If Tip was the bone collector, then he would have been quite familiar with the Union Pacific line in the Como Bluff area east of Medicine Bow, as well as the surrounding country of southern Carbon County. He also may have been looking for work in the late summer of 1878, if he was not already connected with the Union Pacific.

Tip Vincent was born in Jefferson County, Iowa in 1839, the third child of William Vincent, a prosperous farmer.[4] He shows up in Wyoming Territory on the 1870 census as a resident of Green River City in Sweetwater County, where he is listed as a laborer living in the dwelling of James Phillipps. Housed with them was a black barber named John Jackson and another laborer named Lewis Lana.

Phillipps is listed as a boot and shoemaker, but it is unknown what trade Vincent performed, and whether or not he was an assistant to Phillipps. Vincent must have come to Rawlins by 1873 or so where he became a good friend and fishing buddy of soon-to-become lawman James Rankin. Vincent and Rankin joined Jim Nash on a fishing expedition in the upper Snake River country in mid-July 1875,[5] so they already were well acquainted. While in Carbon County, Vincent also became friends with William Daley, Jesse Wallace, and other local Rawlins notables.

If he was a railroad detective by late summer 1878, his familiarity with Rawlins and its people might explain why Superintendent Dickinson assigned him to investigate the incident at the trestle.[6] Based on a current lack of evidence to the contrary, Vincent appears to have been a single man with no immediate family living in the territory.

———

A small, hidden basin sat back in the bluff, above the wooden trestle occupied by the newly arrived Powder River Gang. Dinosaur hunters later named the hidden basin Robbers' Roost for the role it played in the attempted train robbery. This particular bridge trestle was one of only two constructed by the railroad between Medicine Bow and

Como. It would have been much easier to sabotage than the larger, more prominent crossing on the Medicine Bow River itself, which some have identified as the possible crime scene.[7]

Geologist Arthur Lakes confirmed the location of Robbers' Roost in Como Bluff and the wooden trestle below it as the crime scene in his field journal less than a year after the incident. Lakes had been writing notes during his visit to the dinosaur quarries with William Reed while they discussed fossil quarrying and toured geological outcrops. The two men collected some vertebrae from an Ichthyosaurus near what soon became known as Quarry Number Twelve, adjacent to the place Reed referred to as Robbers' Roost. During a rest stop, Reed pointed out the little trestle bridge on the railroad tracks just below when he described the recent crime to Lakes.

Lakes related the story in his journal for May 17, 1879, confident in Reed's knowledge, since the paleontologist was familiar with the terrain, the robbery story, and had been collecting fossils in the Como area at the time of the derailment attempt. A map of Yale University fossil vertebrate localities for 1877–1889 identifies the Robbers' Roost locality in a publication of Lakes's journal, and this map may be the first time that name shows up in print. The crime scene is located near fossil Quarry Number Twelve.[8]

Since the railroad trestle had been visible to the two men just below the roost, my archeological crew was able to locate the same area and investigate the site in 1996 to determine if any evidence remained. A brief survey confirmed evidence of the former crime scene location. A raised railroad grade, overgrown with grasses, was bisected by a shallow drainage emanating from a hidden basin back in the hills, the one known as Robbers' Roost. Fish plates, bent rails, spikes, and wooden trestle posts still exist at the locality, but may postdate the crime. While the posts were rotted off on top, they still were seated firmly in the ground. The wooden structure would have supported the trestle in 1878, when trains still traveled the original railroad alignment.

Parott later admitted the outlaws initially had intended to derail the eastbound train Number Four. This was the same one advertised

Beth Southwell *(foreground)*, Brent Breithaupt, and Rick Weathermon take part in the archaeological investigation at the Como Bluff railroad trestle near Robbers' Roost. *Author photo.*

in the newspaper as the treasure train during the Percy robbery coverage. But Parott's work was thwarted when the train rushed by just as the outlaws were beginning to loosen rails. The engine nearly knocked him off the trestle and down into the shallow ravine.

The unsuccessful desperados rode over the hill into Robbers' Roost and waited until evening to finish loosening the rails, remove fish plates, and prepare for the next train. This alternative plan was to ditch the westbound evening passenger train Number Three and collect any personal valuables the passengers were carrying.

The outlaws tied telegraph wire around the loosened south rail, ran the wire to a nearby hiding place, and lay in wait for Number Three. This technique of train ditching had been employed by the James Gang years earlier, which helps explain Frank James's role and intentions in the Como Bluff crime. McKinney was in charge of the gang at the trestle, and McKinney was an alias used at the time by Frank James, according to Parott. Years earlier Frank and Jesse once pulled a loosened rail just in front of a passing train to derail it in Iowa in the same manner.[9]

A section man named John Brown[10] came by on a railroad handcar during the derailing attempt. He noticed the loosened rail and, according to some accounts, stopped to repair it. However, no mention is made of his noticing the wire wrapped around the rail, and it seems odd that a trained eye would miss it.

Alternatively, Brown may not have stopped long, but noticed the telegraph wire and determined that foul play was intended, so he went back to Como Station as if nothing was amiss, where he reported the incident. Either way, the outlaws now knew they had been detected by railroad authorities, and their presence on the line was a liability before any robbery attempt was completed.

Frank James wanted to shoot Brown at the trestle, but Frank Tole and Parott talked him out of it. Instead, the bandit gang rode toward Elk Mountain to distance themselves from any lawmen who might come to investigate the trestle scene. During the entire episode up to this point, the gang members had not pulled their guns on an innocent person and were guilty only of rail tampering with the intent to rob a train. Things would soon get worse.

According to Big Nose George, the gang arrived at their canyon camp near Elk Mountain on August 18. In a later interview Parott said, "We got into Elk Mountain Sunday afternoon following the time that we took this rail up—the rail was taken up Saturday evening."[11]

Elk Mountain itself stands as a beacon above the surrounding terrain, even while riding horseback at dark, and still is a prominent landmark for orientation. The total distance from the trestle crime scene to the outlaws' camp is about thirty-five miles, a long day's ride for determined outlaws on the run, so they probably needed to rest their horses on arrival at camp.

The outlaws rode the first leg of their escape route in the evening shortly after the robbery attempt, which explains why they initially followed a well-traveled road parallel to the railroad tracks, moving westerly to cross the Medicine Bow River. None of the gang seems to have been very familiar with Carbon County or the Elk Mountain area to which they were now headed, so they moved cautiously trying to avoid detection by anyone in the area.

Coincidentally Undersheriff James Rankin had just delivered two of the earlier Percy train robbers to the Territorial Prison at Laramie and was returning to Rawlins on the Express passenger train the evening of August 17. Rankin typically performed much of the case work for Lawry and was a well-known figure in the county. He also had started a livery business in town that became a successful investment. Although a quiet man, he never seemed to be far away when the county needed law enforcement.

On August 17, Rankin was traveling on the same Number Three train that the outlaws would have derailed if the trestle sabotage had been successful.[12] Instead of finishing their trip to Rawlins, Rankin and his traveling companion J.B. Adams, the UPRR Agent, received a telegram at Rock Creek discussing the loosened rail near Como. The missive asked Rankin to continue on in the Express car to the railroad station at Medicine Bow where another message awaited him. This communique requested that he leave the next morning (Sunday, August 18) with Adams to investigate the trestle bridge where the rails had been tampered with.

Rankin and Adams examined the crime scene along the tracks on Sunday, meeting Albany County Sheriff Nottage and Superintendent Ed Dickinson of the UPRR at the trestle, along with a couple of other men. The group discussed the situation among themselves and seem to have agreed that the tracks of several horses once tied on a hill south of the railroad were unrelated to the men who had attempted the derailment. Nottage went back to Laramie satisfied, while Rankin and Adams rode horseback along the south side of the railroad tracks heading toward Medicine Bow.[13]

After a quarter-mile ride, Rankin discovered a beaten trail made by several horses parallel to the railroad. Rankin was intimately familiar with horses as owner of the stable in Rawlins, and his judgment would have been quite reliable in this instance.[14] He convinced

Adams the tracks were not from loose stock, because loose horses did not leave this kind of a trail.

Realizing the tracks were fresh, he proposed to Adams that they follow them back to the hill near the trestle to find where they had originated. The men backtracked the sign to within about three hundred yards of where Sheriff Nottage had found evidence of horses being tied up. The ground there became so tracked up that the trail could not be followed any farther in that direction. Rankin determined the horses once tied above the trestle were the same ones that made the tracks found a quarter mile west. The physical evidence suggested to him a group of riders had dismounted at the trestle, moved about, then remounted before riding away along the tracks.

Rankin was determined to investigate the horse tracks in spite of J.B. Adams' objection, so they turned back toward Medicine Bow where they first found the trail. They followed the trail about two miles where they crossed the Medicine Bow River and topped a hill in sight of Trabing's store and freighting facilities near Medicine Bow Station. From here, the group of riders ahead of Rankin and Adams left the road and took off in a southwesterly direction away from the community.

At Trabing's, Rankin and Adams inquired if anyone had noticed several riders in the vicinity the previous evening. No one had. Adams again suggested they return to Medicine Bow, but Rankin wanted to continue the search a bit farther. It had rained about five hours the night before, leaving damp earth on the trail and distinctive hoofprints in the soft ground. Rankin may have realized the hoofprints were set deeper in the earth than those expected for a lighter, riderless horse on its way to water. Besides, loose horses heading to water would stop at the river to drink rather than parallel it for miles.

The two men continued another four miles southwesterly, indicating to Rankin the general area where the trail was headed. He could tell the gang's route would pass about five miles southeast of the small coal town of Carbon. Rankin and Adams had ridden about nine miles southwest of the crime scene when Rankin finally agreed to return to Medicine Bow. Once there, the two men took a switch engine to Carbon where Adams telegraphed UPRR authorities about the trail discovery and sought further input.

Rankin, Adams, Isaac Fieldhouse, and Deputy Sheriff Robert Widdowfield rode south from Carbon later that day for about five-and-a-half miles until they found the outlaws' trail once again, somewhere east of Simpson Ridge and west of Sand Creek. It followed the main road for half a mile before it took off directly west through the sagebrush.

Robert Widdowfield was thirty-two years old in 1878 and served as Ike Lawry's deputy from the coal town of Carbon. He had a wife and family living there, and some of his descendants still lived in the county in the 1990s.[15] Widdowfield had honed his tracking skills during the Percy manhunt earlier that year, talents he now needed to follow the suspected trail they were on.

Once they relocated the trail, Widdowfield and the three others moved through the brush for four more miles to the foot of a hill where one set of horse tracks led up the hill on one side, while seven others climbed it from the other side. Then a heavy rain began to fall, blinding the trail when Widdowfield and the others topped the hill.

The men had difficulty following the dispersed tracks in the harsh elements, but still rode to within two miles of Foote's ranch near Elk Mountain. They left the trail there, and took the road north to the railroad town of Percy, arriving about sundown on Sunday, August 18. After reporting in, Rankin ordered a handcar from the railroad sent as far as Simpson to see if the horse trail had crossed the railroad tracks. It had not.

Deputy Widdowfield knew this country well and told the others he thought he knew right where the horsemen might camp. After all, this was his home country. Union Pacific Superintendent Ed Dickinson arrived at Percy from Rawlins that evening along with Carbon County Sheriff Ike Lawry, who brought Tip Vincent to help Widdowfield continue tracking the next day. Vincent was employed by Dickinson as a railroad agent.[16] Rankin briefed Vincent and Widdowfield, the two new trackers, about the situation, and the group gave them instructions for the following day.

Rattlesnake Canyon is heavily timbered, Elk Mountain is in the background. *Author photo.*

Judging from the evidence, one of the outlaws' horses had been wearing shoes fitted with oversized metal corks. Corks are the pegs or caulks screwed into the ground surface of the horseshoe's back end to serve as cleats and give the horse added traction in rough country. Large corks make a distinct signature track with deep indents in the ground from each hoofprint, and this may have aided Rankin in identifying the correct trail in the soft earth. Unique tracks would facilitate staying on course during their reconnaissance. If a distinguishing set of tracks was observed, Rankin would have relayed this evidence to those who took over tracking duties the next day.

Rankin and Adams stayed overnight in Percy, resting there until Monday morning, August 19. Widdowfield and Vincent took off together that morning to pick up the horse trail, posing as ranchers riding the range in search of livestock so as not to raise suspicion in any quarter. Rankin eventually returned to Rawlins.

No firsthand testimony exists for Widdowfield and Vincent's movements before they discovered the outlaws' camp, but they must have ridden south to pick up the outlaws' trail where the lawmen had left it the day before. This was a simple process since Widdowfield had been riding with Rankin on Sunday evening. Both Widdowfield and Vincent were good trackers, familiar with the terrain of southern Carbon County, and deliberate men who knew how to finish a job. They would have made good time once they cut the outlaws' trail.

Detailed scrutiny of Holt's 1883 map of Wyoming and relevant GLO maps, indicate where the trackers might have picked up the trail two miles short of Foote's ranch along the old Overland Stage Road. From there, the outlaws ahead of the lawmen skirted Foote's place to the northwest to avoid his fenced pasture, and soon reached the well-traveled wagon road west of the ranch.

Historian Meschter, in his book, outlines a slightly different route for this segment, and his thorough research makes some valuable points.[17] Presumably the outlaws' trail then split off the Overland Stage Road about a mile west of Foote's, and crossed the hills southwest of Rattlesnake Pass before it descended to the banks of Rattlesnake Creek a mile and a half above the Overland Trail.[18]

The renegades then turned upstream along a cattle trail and headed south into the canyon for two-and-a-half miles where they made camp late on August 18. They camped near the divide at the head of Rattlesnake Creek, where the terrain beyond drops down south into the Pass Creek country. Friends and relatives of Widdowfield eventually marked the location of the camp with a monument in the late nineteenth century, so the terminus of the outlaws' trail is not in dispute today. A brief archaeological survey in the 1990s confirmed its location.

Big Nose George later recalled that the outlaws fashioned a makeshift wickiup in the trees near the mouth of the canyon half a mile below camp, so one of their members could keep an eye out for approaching riders. The rest of the gang rode up the canyon, built a couple of fires, and settled in to rest for the evening.

On the morning of August 19, the guard in the wickiup noticed two horses heading his way. They first looked like loose stock in the distance, but the moving figures soon proved to be mounted riders. The guard doused his small campfire at the wickiup and galloped

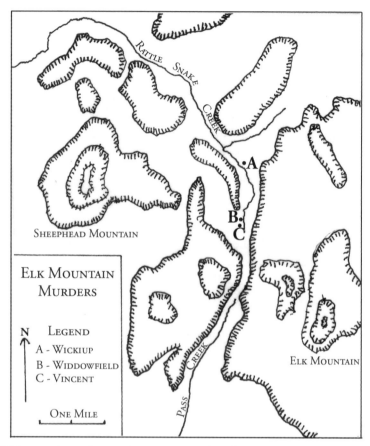

This map shows the murder scene in Rattlesnake Canyon. *By author.*

to where the other men rested in camp. One of the outlaws there had just reshod his horse after breaking off the long metal corks, and the pieces of discarded iron lay scattered about the camp.[19] This man's horse was the one that had made distinctive hoofprints in the trail after they left the railroad trestle near Como Bluff.

Both Rankin and Adams had known early on they were following shod horse tracks pressed into the ground by the weight of several riders. In fact, when the tracks struck wet soil, Rankin probably could isolate each set of tracks and estimate the number of men in the party. At any rate, the two investigators knew they would be outnumbered by the riders ahead of them, so that helps explain their overnight stop at Percy. It is fortunate they never met up with the outlaws on the trail, but Widdowfield and Vincent were not so lucky, even though they must have been briefed on the suspected large number of riders in the outlaws' party.

Authorities at Percy on the night of August 18 would have been clear in their instructions to Widdowfield and Vincent, emphasizing the numerical superiority of the riders ahead of them. If the two trackers spotted the suspects ahead on the trail, then one should hurry for reinforcements while the other kept the outlaws under surveillance.

Minimal aspen leaves had fallen by August, so Widdowfield and Vincent easily tracked the well-marked trail up Rattlesnake Canyon and into the timber. The trail led across the creek and over to a small clearing with two campfires in plain view, one of which was still smoldering.

The scene looked to the lawmen like a recently abandoned camp, rather than the setting for a dangerous trap. Widdowfield decided to test the temperature of the ashes to estimate how far ahead in time and distance the riders might be. He had no idea they were as close as they were or that the outlaws' horses were hidden in the nearby trees.

Once the outlaws had been alerted to oncoming riders, they cleaned up camp, doused the fires, and hid in the trees and bushes twenty feet away. They agreed that if the two riders were just cattlemen out looking for livestock, they would let them pass by unmolested. Widdowfield and Vincent rode up the canyon on the east bank of Rattlesnake Creek and saw the campfires on the other side. Both riders then crossed the creek, which was dry in some places as the late summer water frequently ran beneath the layer of jumbled rocks scattered along its bed.

Widdowfield stopped his horse at the largest campfire, dismounted, and walked over to the coals. Vincent said to him, "I guess our stock ain't here,"[20] which suggests Vincent suspected the outlaws were nearby and wanted to maintain their ruse as stockmen.

This body at the murder scene is believed to have been staged during the investigation. *Courtesy, Carbon County Museum, Rawlins, Wyoming.*

But Widdowfield commented to Vincent that the coals were hot as hell, so the outlaws couldn't be too far away. This statement convinced the outlaws of the riders' intentions, and Frank Tole, who had kept a bead on Widdowfield when he dismounted, instantly shot Widdowfield in the face. The deputy landed dead in the ashes.

Other outlaws concealed in the foliage realized when Widdowfield spoke to Vincent that the two men were lawmen tracking them. If they didn't kill them both right away, the two deputies would track the horses into the trees and uncover the outlaws' hiding place. Frank Tole had made the first decision to fire, and the rest of the gang followed suit.

Robert Widdowfield's coroner's inquest[21] indicates he was shot with a rifle later found blood-splattered, just a few steps away from his body. This weapon may have been Dutch Charley's Springfield carbine, which would implicate him in the actual murder instead of Frank Tole. Widdowfield's body was found covered in brush, lying with the left side of his shattered face pointing down. The back part of his scalp had been blown away by the gunshot, and the right side of his hair was scorched above the ear.

Someone took a photo of a prone human body along Rattlesnake Creek at the time the posse later found the murdered lawmen. The body closely fits the description of Widdowfield's corpse, but it does not agree completely with his description in the coroner's inquest. This discrepancy has led some to believe one of the posse members may have later posed in the photo to demonstrate the general nature of the crime scene. Some wonder if the actor was I.C. Miller[22] who later became the county sheriff in 1880, but this has not been confirmed.

Henry Vincent was still mounted when Widdowfield fell. He yanked his horse to attention just as the outlaws emerged from the trees and fired a first volley at him. Vincent may have taken a round or two in the thigh when he turned his mount up the canyon to escape the fusillade. Seemingly the volley wasn't angled properly to hit a rider on horseback, so the outlaws ran from their concealment to get a better bead on the rider. They fired a second volley at Vincent as he rode away with his back toward them.

One particularly accurate round struck Vincent in the back and exited through his chest, knocking him off his horse. He probably couldn't have ridden more than fifty yards during this unfolding terror. He rose to his knees as his mount bolted away, aimed his revolver at the outlaws, and tried returning fire.

When the outlaw gang fired a third volley, two additional rounds entered Vincent's torso, and he fell dead in front of the gang. About twenty total shots had been fired altogether, and Big Nose George later admitted that he had done as much shooting at Vincent as any one of the outlaws.

Several gang members robbed the dead bodies right after the murders. Someone took Vincent's boots and gun, then put a strap around one of his legs to drag him into the creek bed and cover him up with old brush. One of Vincent's guns may have been a rifle given to him by Sir John Reed as payment for scouting services Tip performed while Reed was exploring in Wyoming.[23] Dutch Charley discarded his fifty-caliber Springfield carbine at the campsite and stole a Sharps that belonged to Widdowfield. Widdowfield's body also was dragged into the creek bed and covered with brush, but apparently was not robbed of anything other than his Sharps.

Between August and September 1878, L.M. Lampton had been surveying the township in which the murders occurred for the General Land Office. He recalled hearing about twenty shots fired somewhere in Rattlesnake Canyon on the day in question.[24] This serves as independent confirmation of the date of death.

The two trackers were murdered on Monday, August 19, 1878, the first double homicide of law enforcement officers killed in the line of duty in Wyoming Territory. The first victim in the territory had been Deputy Sheriff Adolph Cuny of the Laramie County Sheriff's Office, shot dead on July 22, 1877. Widdowfield became the second and Vincent the third officer to die while serving the people of Wyoming Territory.[25]

The outlaws stayed in their Rattlesnake Canyon camp a while longer to hide evidence of their crime, then rode together for only a short distance before splitting up to take separate routes back to the Powder River country and elsewhere. Frank Tole left the gang right after the murders and traveled on his own circuitous route back toward the Black Hills.

The *Laramie Daily Sentinel*[26] picked up the story several days after the incident, since Rawlins had no newspaper that year. At first, the Laramie paper thought the story of the train derailment was pure fiction, explaining that the disturbed rails only suggested workmen repairing the trestle. They also argued the horse tracks near the crime scene were the product of loose stock searching for water.

Three days later, they were more convinced of the story's accuracy and mentioned that two expert scouts had been dispatched to follow the trail first located by Rankin and Adams.[27] The two law enforcement officers themselves had not reported in since leaving Percy on Monday morning, August 19.

The sketches show relevant brands. Horses 1, 2, and 3 were running loose near Elk Mountain after the murders. Horse 4 appears in a later sketch of Big Nose George's lynching. *Illustration by author.*

On Sunday, August 25, authorities sent out a scouting party to look for the missing lawmen.[28] Reportedly, this posse encountered a couple of hunters near Elk Mountain who had previously seen eight horsemen going into Rattlesnake Canyon, followed later by two additional riders. They then heard firing, followed by seven horsemen leading one riderless horse while coming out of the canyon. This scenario may be explained by the likelihood that the outlaws caught Widdowfield's horse, and Tole already had left the group.

A lone saddled horse with bridle and lariat was seen running loose near Medicine Bow on Monday, August 26, one week after the murders. A tin cup and mask dangled from the saddle horn.

Two additional men joined the search for the deputies that same day. The UPRR armed their trains to provide added protection to passengers with the outlaws still at large. Authorities told people to keep an eye out for loose horses that may have belonged to the missing officers. They mentioned three branded horses. One missing animal was described as a dark gray mare, branded "HL" on the fore shoulder and "A" on the left hip. The mount carried a heavy California saddle, light gray blanket, and new bridle. A second animal was a light gray mare, eight years old, branded "OC" on the left hip, with an anchor and cross on the left shoulder. This second horse wore a newly leathered California saddle with hand-holds on the hind tree. A third horse was described as a bay mare, branded "CB" on her left shoulder, with a white spot on the forehead, heavily built, with lots of saddle marks, but no saddle.[29]

Carbon County brand records for 1872–1881 do not list either Vincent or Widdowfield with a registered horse brand, although Robert's brother, Joseph Widdowfield, did register an unrelated brand.[30] Those records state that some brands existed in the county that have never been recorded before, so formal transfers were not necessary whenever the brands changed hands. It is possible, then, that neither Widdowfield nor Vincent ever registered their horse brands, so no records exist. They also may not have owned any other branded livestock.

Curiously saddled and bareback horses seem to have run loose between Medicine Bow and Elk Mountain in the days following the Widdowfield/Vincent murders. Abundant mayhem and confusion reigned throughout southern Carbon County due to the mysterious circumstances. Residents worried about the current state of affairs and wanted to know where were Widdowfield and Vincent?

The train robbery at Como Bluff had been an abject failure. Two lawmen sent on the trail of the outlaws were still missing. Nervous horses ran riderless all over the country. And the criminals from Powder River had disappeared in the billowing dust of countless Wyoming trails.

Chapter Three

Outlaw Diaspora

NOBODY WITNESSED the Elk Mountain murders in Rattlesnake Canyon other than the eight perpetrators and two victims, which made it fairly simple for the outlaws to disperse into the remote countryside and avoid any immediate pursuit by law enforcement. If only each murderer had kept his mouth shut from there on out, no one ever would have had any reason to connect these troubled souls with the Widdowfield/Vincent homicides. Authorities did not even know the two lawmen were dead until over a week after their murders, and it was not until much later that they learned the names of the outlaws suspected.

Frank Tole had been one of the murderers, and almost certainly he pulled the trigger on the rifle that killed Widdowfield. His ongoing descent into violence escalated after he left the woodcutting job for Brock near the first site of Fort McKinney earlier that spring. He had been an accomplished criminal even before he worked for Brock, and honest work did not abide by the man after he left. Tole was the first to turn violent along Rattlesnake Creek when Widdowfield touched the campfire embers, and his spontaneous response converted the Powder River Gang from a group of unsuccessful train robbers into felony murderers.

Tole traveled quickly on his own after leaving the Elk Mountain crime scene once the deed was done. By September 1878, less than a month after he shot Robert Widdowfield in the face, he operated again as a road agent along the Black Hills stage route. He joined a

This monument reads: Rob Widdowfield/Of Carbon Wyo/And Tip Vincent/Of Rawlins Wyo/Murdered here/August 19, 1878. It was erected by Widdowfield's friends and relatives at the murder scene. *Author photo.*

gang of six men that robbed the northbound coach at Old Woman's Fork of the Cheyenne River about eleven in the evening of September 13, but the outlaws weren't finished with their plans.

Suspecting a similar attempt would be made by Tole's gang on the upcoming southbound coach, Boone May and John Zimmerman rode a couple hundred yards behind the stage to protect it on its journey toward Cheyenne.[1] Tole and his road agents did stop the coach as expected and were rifling through the passengers' possessions after setting the mail sacks on the ground. May and Zimmerman rode into the scene with shotguns blazing, and Tole fell mortally wounded. Two of the outlaw's compadres later returned to the location when it was safe and buried his body nearby. The first of the

This vicinity of the Black Hills stage route provides many opportunities for ambush. *Author photo.*

Widdowfield and Vincent murderers was dead, the man who had fired the first shot.

Tole's body was buried before authorities even knew he had been one of the outlaws involved in the Elk Mountain murders. His name had not yet been revealed to the citizenry, and only a few outlaws knew of his role. But additional news would emerge regarding Frank Tole not long after his death.

Elsewhere, a separate gang of road agents gathered in December 1878, near the small cow town of Rock Creek along the Union Pacific fifty miles west of Laramie. Some of these bad men were acquainted with a couple of the outlaws who had been in the Powder

River Gang; apparently outlawry was a small but fluid fraternity. Local citizens from Rock Creek grew concerned that the outlaws hidden in the hills were planning to steal the soldier payroll due in town shortly by rail, destined for the Fort Fetterman garrison.[2] Recently elected Albany County Sheriff N.K. Boswell was dispatched as a special detective to investigate the region and rid it of any bandits who might be preparing a holdup.

The encamped outlaws sent one of their number, Frank Howard, to town to gather supplies for the group, but Howard got cold feet regarding their scheme and instead tipped off authorities about the outlaws' plans. This was the same Frank Howard who had ridden with Dutch Charley earlier in the year up in Powder River country when they picked up Frank Tole at Brock's woodcutting camp.

Boswell coordinated with Ed Dickinson of the UPRR to get a posse together and a special rail car for the trip to Rock Creek. The train pulled into the station about ten the evening of December 22, 1878, where a man named Thayer met them with fresh horses and directions to the outlaws' camp that Howard had divulged to him.[3]

The posse initially rode a quiet trail to the camp, but found it recently abandoned. They then headed to a nearby cabin to question the owner about his knowledge of the outlaws' whereabouts and their choice for a new camp. Authorities suspected the man to be a spotter for the outlaws. With new information obtained from him, the lawmen found and encircled the sleeping camp, moved in with weapons drawn, and held the startled outlaws at gunpoint, making them raise their hands as they climbed from their bedrolls.

The Rock Creek outlaws were a motley crew, but none had been in on the Elk Mountain murders. One of its members was Joe Minuse, who had been in Brown's Park, Colorado, looking to gather fresh horses for the Powder River Gang when they tried robbing the train at Como Bluff in August, but he got delayed in the process. Fortunately for him, he did not meet up with Frank James and Big Nose George in time to take part in the Vincent and Widdowfield murders. His tardiness saved his neck from the gallows. The other bandits captured with Minuse at Rock Creek were Henry Harrington, Frederick Robie, Frank Howard (the informant), and Charles "the Kid" Condon.[4]

When Boswell's posse found Harrington in the camp, he had Robert Widdowfield's heavy California saddle, so the officers suspected these outlaws might know something about the Elk Mountain murders. The sheriff coaxed information from Minuse once they were back in Laramie where Boswell stretched the outlaw's neck with the end of a rope until he began to talk. Some of Minuse's information seems a bit disjointed in Pence's account of Boswell,[5] but other tidbits advance our knowledge of the Powder River Gang after their split.

Apparently, the Como Bluff train robbery attempt had been McKinney's (Frank James) idea. Minuse claimed it was Dutch Charley who killed Widdowfield, and it may have been Dutch's carbine left at the scene that did the deed. But, Minuse was not present in Rattlesnake Canyon to witness the murders. He must have gotten his information from someone who had been there, probably Dutch Charley himself. Dutch Charley may have bragged about his role in the crime and overstated his involvement because it was Tole who shot Widdowfield.

Dutch Charley had visited the Rock Creek camp shortly before Boswell's posse invaded it, and that is when he gave Widdowfield's saddle to Harrington. Minuse talked with Dutch Charley in the camp at that time, and this may have been when details about the two murders were first transmitted outside the Powder River Gang. Minuse eventually revealed for the first time to authorities the identity of the eight outlaws who took part in the Elk Mountain murders.[6] At last, their names and descriptions could be circulated to other lawmen in other communities and rewards offered for their arrest and conviction. The manhunt began in earnest.

According to Dutch Charley's conversations with both Minuse and Frank Howard, the gang from Powder River had often quarreled among themselves beginning with the debate over killing handcar operator John Brown at the Como Bluff trestle. Rancor worsened after the two deputies were murdered along Rattlesnake Creek, so the gang decided to split up and go their separate ways.

Frank Tole rode to his death at the Black Hills stage holdup shortly after the Elk Mountain affair. Tom Reed may have ridden out alone as well. Big Nose George took off to the north, probably accompanied by Jack Campbell and John Wells. Frank James and Sim Wan left together. Some people thought Sim Wan was Jesse James, but this probably was not the case as Jesse was never indicted for the Elk Mountain crimes.

Dutch Charley made it to Rock Creek where he eventually met up with Joe Minuse, Frank Howard, and the other outlaws present. But Charley left for Green River just before Frank Howard went into town to get food for those planning a heist of the soldier payroll. His exit saved him from arrest in the Rock Creek camp.

While Harrington ended up with Widdowfield's saddle, Dutch Charley kept Widdowfield's horse since his mount had worn out and was running loose after the murders. Vincent's horse had taken off after the lawman's bullet-riddled body hit the ground along Rattlesnake Creek, and the animal was not captured by the outlaw gang. The animal may have escaped over the divide down into Pass Creek.

Public opinion boiled in Carbon County when they heard the names of the perpetrators who murdered the two popular law enforcement officers. The masses screamed for justice. When news arrived from Rock Creek that Dutch Charley had been one of the murderers and was recently with that outlaw gang, Sheriff Boswell decided it was time to find and arrest him. Frank Howard and Henry Harrington turned state's evidence to assist in the manhunt process and hopefully avoid serious jail time themselves.[7]

Frank Howard traveled with Albany County Deputy John Lefever and others on New Year's Eve 1878 to arrest Dutch Charley at a Green River saloon.[8] Howard recognized the outlaw in the bar crowd, pointed him out to Lefever, then helped guard the prisoner on the train back to Laramie that evening. Dutch Charley must have hated Howard for turning on him in the saloon. When the

Rock foundations mark the site of the town of Carbon today. *Courtesy, Todd Surovell, Department of Anthropology, University of Wyoming.*

group reached Laramie, Howard and the other officers left Charley in the charge of soon-to-be sworn-in Sheriff N.K. Boswell.[9]

Carbon County got wind of the outlaw being held in Laramie and requested he be sent to Rawlins to stand trial for murder. Rawlins authorities had not yet prepared indictments, but they had Dutch Charley's admission to the Rock Creek outlaws regarding his complicity in the Elk Mountain murders.

Boswell placed Albany County deputy Sheriff Ed Kearns in charge of moving the prisoner along the UPRR to the Carbon County seat.[10] Suspecting trouble in the town of Carbon where Widdowfield had lived and where he still had family, Kerns hid Dutch Charley behind some trunks in the baggage car as they pulled into town.[11]

Restless citizens from the coal town were somehow made aware that the prisoner was being moved through their community on the cold evening of Sunday, January 5, 1879. Local relatives of Robert Widdowfield were particularly agitated. A crowd of about one hundred citizens gathered at the railroad station when Passenger Train Number Three carrying Dutch Charley arrived, and they grabbed the prisoner after overpowering the authorities. The crowd took him to a telegraph pole in front of Beckwith and Quinn's store where they fitted a hangman's noose around his neck about 9:30 P.M.[12]

Joe Minuse, ca. 1879, was tried and found innocent of shooting Tip Vincent. *Courtesy, Nebraska State Historical Society, photograph collections.*

Masked men stood the hatless outlaw up on a board several feet above the ground with his neck still in the noose. At first Dutch Charley denied knowing anything about the Elk Mountain murders, calling himself Charley Bates. He then asked for a fair trial where he would help expose the rest of the gang members already named by Minuse. When he realized he was going to be killed by the crowd, he asked to be shot instead of hanged. His request was ignored and he was hanged, dangling there until about three the next afternoon, January 6, according to Jens Hanson, an eyewitness to the lynching.[13] Afterward, a bottle of medicine taken from the dead man's pocket was seen to be labeled with the name "Charles Bates."[14] A second gang member was dead.

Hanson cut the body down, took it to the train depot, and helped the coroner put it on the Express to Rawlins where the inquest would be held. Hanson's testimony at the inquest in Rawlins identified the body there as the same man he had cut down at Carbon the day before.

George W. English also testified at Dutch Charley's coroner's inquest, stating he had first met the outlaw about July 25, 1878, on Crazy Woman Fork in the Powder River country. Dutch Charley already had a reputation as a horse thief by then and had ridden into English's camp. English believed the outlaw to be about twenty-two years old at the time they met. July 25 was the same day as the mail robbery attempt on the Deadwood line that may have involved Dutch Charley, so English's time estimate was off a couple of days.

Authorities held Dutch Charley's coroner's inquest on January 7, 1879, after his body arrived in Rawlins from Carbon on the Union Pacific.[15] But, local legend in the country around Carbon recounts that after he was cut down from the telegraph pole in that town, he was buried outside the fence bordering the Carbon Cemetery; the same cemetery that contains the mortal remains of Robert Widdowfield and other citizens. This scenario is unlikely.

Court documents prove his body was hauled to Rawlins for the inquest, and it is doubtful anyone went to the trouble to haul him back to Carbon for burial. Rather his body probably was put in a pauper's grave in Rawlins or may have been discarded somewhere along the railroad line in southern Wyoming. He was so hated by the citizenry he was not likely given any deference when his body was discarded.

Carbon County's legal machinery kicked into high gear after Dutch Charley's death. Joe Minuse had been in custody for several months since the Rock Creek raid, and an official criminal complaint was filed against him on March 31, 1879, stating that Minuse had fired a rifle into the chest of Henry H. Vincent, killing him instantly.[16] It was signed by Carbon County Prosecuting Attorney, G.C. Smith and sworn to by J.R. Hawley, Carbon County Justice of the Peace. By April 7, 1879, Rawlins was ready to bring Minuse to trial for his alleged role in the murder of Henry Vincent.[17]

County authorities filed the murder indictment as Criminal Case Number 265, naming Joe (John) Minuse, Big Nose George Parott,

Frank James, John Wells, Sim Wan, Jack Campbell, and Tim (Tom) Reed as partners in the homicide.[18] The indictment also listed Frank Tole and Dutch Charley, but their names were marked out on the document since they already were dead.

The text of that indictment is telling. It contrasts with the March 31 complaint against Minuse by stating that it was Big Nose George who used a rifle to shoot Vincent in the breast near the heart and lungs, leaving a half-inch diameter wound that instantly killed the officer. The other named outlaws were proclaimed accomplices in the murder.

Whoever fired the shot that killed Vincent, it must have been after the second volley of gunfire that wounded Vincent and caused him to fall from his horse then face the outlaws as he raised his own gun. Otherwise, Vincent's back would have been turned toward the outlaws and any shot couldn't enter his breast, only exit there. If the shot in question killed Vincent instantly, it must have been during the third and final volley when Vincent was the greatest distance away from the gang and turned to face them. If Parott actually pulled the trigger, as the Territory of Wyoming argued, then it is understandable why county citizens were so eager to have him brought to justice.

Witnesses were subpoenaed and a jury trial for Minuse set for September 9, 1879, in District Court in Rawlins. Joe Minuse testified that he was indeed the man indicted for the murder of Henry Vincent and Robert Widdowfield, but he was without means to make his defense, wanting to call witnesses on his behalf.[19] These witnesses were W.A. Johnson, A. Hanson, L.L. Crocholt, Charles Davis, A. McIntosh, and Walter Frank. The Court document was signed by John Manuse, a spelling variant for his name.

After a short one-day trial, the jury returned their verdict: "We the Jury in the case of the Territory of Wyoming versus John Minuse, find the Defendant *Not Guilty* as charged in the Indictment."[20] It was signed on September 10, 1879, by Wm. Brauer, Foreman. No evidence could prove Minuse had been involved in the murders. After his acquittal, he was arrested in Green River for horse stealing and later released on December 24, 1881, after serving two years in confinement for that offense.[21]

Carbon County authorities prepared additional murder indictments on April 7, 1879, after the one for Joe Minuse. His indictment in Criminal Case Number 265 would be used a year and a half later when one of the Powder River Gang stood trial for the murder of Henry Vincent, even though these other indictments also had been drafted.

In addition to Henry Vincent's murder, indictments were handed down on the same day for the murder of Robert Widdowfield, Criminal Case Number 266.[22] Accused in that document were John Minuse (alias Joe Minuse), George Parott (alias Big Nose George), Frank James (alias McKinney), John Wells (alias Sandy), Sim Wan, Jack Campbell, Tim Reed, Frank Tole, and Charles Bates (alias Dutch Charley or One-Winged Charley). Once again, Tole and Dutch Charley were dead, so their names were scratched out.

Authorities listed Frank Tole as the man who pulled the trigger on Widdowfield, shooting the lawman in the head. But since Tole's name is scratched out, Tom Reed (earlier identified as Tim Reed) was now listed as the shooter. This maneuver perhaps reflects the common knowledge that Tole was dead, and authorities wanted to indict a living suspect.

Criminal Case Number 271 listed a second indictment for the murder of Henry H. Vincent. Minuse, Parott, James, Wells, Wan, Campbell, and Reed were named once again.[23] Tole and Dutch Charley were completely absent this time, but the indictment added a Charles Torrey for whom a bench warrant had been issued. Torrey stated in an affidavit filed September 11, 1879, that he was the man indicted with the others for the Elk Mountain murders, but had no means to support a defense that required testimony from James Pinkham and John Doe (C.G. Thorp).

These witnesses were subpoenaed, and Torrey proved to be innocent of the charges.[24] It is possible, although unlikely, the addition of his name to Criminal Case Number 271 was simply a mistaken reference to Charley Bates (Dutch Charley). At any rate, no further action seems to have been taken against Torrey, and nothing more is known about him or why he was suspected of the crime.

Interestingly, Frank James was listed in Criminal Case Number 271 as the man who shot a rifle into Henry Vincent, the bullet penetrating near the heart and lungs. So much public attention was now focused on the named murderers, it is lucky for them they had headed out in all directions after leaving Elk Mountain.

If Frank James and Sim Wan actually left the Powder River Gang together on August 19, 1878, they must have split up shortly afterward, because Frank rode through southwestern Wyoming that fall and settled at a ranch near Bitter Creek called the Circle K.[25] His brother Jesse ostensibly joined him a bit later with plans to spend the winter of 1878-1879 there. The likelihood that Frank left the Powder River Gang with Sim Wan, and the fact that Jesse showed up soon after at the Circle K, may have given rise to un-substantiated speculation that Sim Wan and Jesse James were the same person.

Once Frank and Jesse settled at the ranch, they could rest fairly easy so far away from the long arm reach of the law. The two brothers nearly froze to death a few months later while at a cabin on Henry's Fork in March 1879. They may have learned at that time about the criminal complaint against Joe Minuse. Both men must have been relieved to finally vacate the frigid country in April 1879, and return to their old haunts back east. Frank possibly heard of the indictment against him for the murder of Vincent issued that same month and was glad to leave Wyoming Territory.

Frank James maintained a criminal career elsewhere after leaving Wyoming, but surrendered to Missouri authorities in 1882 following his brother Jesse's murder at the hands of Bob Ford earlier that year. Frank spent a little over a year in jail awaiting trial for the October 1879 murder of Frank McMillen during a Missouri train robbery. When his "trial of the century" did take place in Gallatin, Missouri, Frank benefitted from a powerful legal defense team and public sympathy toward the family following Jesse's cruel demise. He was exonerated of all charges against him.[26]

Frank James's name remained on murder indictments in Wyoming Territory, but this fact didn't affect his Missouri prosecution one bit. He never faced justice either for the train derailment near Como Bluff or for his alleged role in the brutal murders of Vincent and Widdowfield near Elk Mountain. Carbon County authorities did not pursue him like they did some others in the gang, and no requisition from Wyoming's governor appears to have been sent to extradite Frank James to Wyoming Territory. James survived unscathed as one of the luckiest members of the gang.

Thomas Reed's name appears as a man held for safekeeping by the U.S. Marshal in Laramie on January 9, 1879, just days after Dutch Charley was hanged. Reed remained in custody at the Territorial Penitentiary outside Laramie until the next term of Court, charged with Larceny of the U.S. Mails.[27] Authorities held his trial on February 5, 1879, where he was acquitted of the crime for which he was arrested and released from custody fifteen days later. This man may or may not have been the same Tom Reed who took part in the Elk Mountain murders. He seems then to have disappeared and remains one of the more mysterious members of the gang.

Sim Wan never faced justice for the murders either. In May 1885, a man thought to be Sim Wan was captured in Montana and placed in a Miles City jail. But, when he was brought south to Laramie, N.K. Boswell proved he was not the Carbon County outlaw. In fact, he was Conrad Heilig, employed on Frank Ketchum's ranch near Cheyenne at the time of the Elk Mountain murders.[28] The real Sim Wan never was caught, and by 1885 the entire trail grew cold.

Big Nose George Parott had left the Elk Mountain country on August 19, 1878, traveling with Jack Campbell and John Wells, eventually heading north toward the Powder River country. By all accounts, they stayed active in outlaw matters. According to historian Doug Engebretson,[29] Parott may have participated in the Canyon Springs holdup of September 28, 1878, near Four Corners, Wyoming, a stage stop on the Cheyenne-Black Hills stage route near the Bear Lodge Mountains.

This Charlie Russell pen-and-ink drawing featured a $1000 reward for Big Nose George who is shown holding up the stage. It was sold as a postcard and is configured similar to the cover art. *Charles M. Russell, 1915.*

The artist Charlie Russell depicted Big Nose George as a holdup man in some of his paintings on the subject of the Cheyenne-Black Hills stage route. In one illustration, a reward notice for Parott is nailed to a tree in the background, while Parott holds a shotgun on the stage driver. This scene possibly used details provided by the actual experiences of a friend of Russell's.[30]

In February 1879, Morris Cahn was carrying a large sum of money on the road between Miles City, Montana, and Bismarck, North Dakota, supported by a small army detachment. The wagon and escort were held up at a place now known as Cahn's Coulee, though not a shot was fired. Holdups during this period netted Big Nose George and his gang tens of thousands of dollars, which, according to legend, he stashed undiscovered somewhere around North Pumpkin Butte.

A bit later, Sheriff Tom Irvine of Custer County, Montana, recognized Big Nose George from the description on wanted posters circulated for the murderers of Robert Widdowfield and Tip Vincent.[31] Irvine took Parott into custody, but nobody arrived in time to make a positive identification so he released the prisoner. It is unknown what likeness of the outlaw was illustrated on the posters, if any, because the only known photograph of Parott seems to have been taken much later in Omaha, Nebraska.

Parott's gang moved to the Sun River country of Montana after his release by Irvine, where they worked on local ranches and used their spare time to plan a heist of the military payroll. Jack Campbell, still riding with Big Nose George, got liquored up one night and spouted out their plan within ear shot of saloon proprietor Johnny Devine. Devine quickly rode to warn the Army authorities, who sent an escort that thwarted the scheme.[32]

Back in Wyoming, Parott and his gang made another abortive attempt at robbing a military payroll between Medicine Bow and Fort Fetterman. Then in South Pass City, Parott allegedly shot and killed cowboy Tom Albro over a disputed poker game, but this has not been confirmed.[33] This murder may be one of the fanciful legends which grew around the life of George Parott.

Near Fort McKinney, Big Nose George and a man named Carey, who may have been Parott's old partner Jack Campbell, rummaged through the contents of Old Man Hill's camp looking for food and valuables.[34] However, author Throgmorton's research shows that Parott, Campbell, and Carey actually rode together at times, so Carey and Campbell could not be the same person.[35]

Apparently, the outlaws were suffering for sustenance by now. However, their plight seems inconsistent with the theory that Parott had stashed thousands of dollars near Pumpkin Buttes.[36] If he was becoming destitute, why wouldn't he just collect some of his stolen loot to buy grub?

Then, in spite of the prices on their heads posted for the Elk Mountain murders, they returned to Miles City, Montana, leading a string of stolen horses, and hoping for better times. Sheriff Tom Irvine was aware of their return and determined to capture and hold Parott this time. He deputized Lew Wilson and Fred Schmalsle to make the arrest. Parott had sequestered himself in the cabin of John Shinnick, probably the brother of Al Shinnick his old riding partner. Campbell stayed out on the town carousing, but both he and Parott were arrested by deputies without incident.

Carbon County received word in April 1880 that Big Nose George had been seen around Miles City, Montana, and later apprehended. Governor of Wyoming John W. Hoyt signed a requisition to the Governor of Montana to have Big Nose George and Jack Campbell brought to Wyoming Territory where they could stand trial for murder. Sheriff James Rankin was charged with bringing the outlaws back. A later requisition also was prepared for John Wells (Sandy), but for some reason he was never apprehended by Rankin, or if he was arrested, he got away.[37]

Jack Campbell is one more outlaw of whom little is known. Meschter, in his book writes the man arrested with Big Nose George was not Jack Campbell, but Bill Carey, and other sources agree.[38] When Rankin arrived in Miles City and questioned the man named Carey, he was satisfied that only Big Nose George was wanted for the Elk Mountain murders.

Parott, Campbell, and Wells apparently had ridden together in southern Montana after the Elk Mountain murders, so they probably escaped Rattlesnake Creek together in August 1878. In any case, Campbell is not heard from again. Carbon County took no further action against him or any of the Elk Mountain outlaws after Big Nose George.

Once Sheriff Rankin knew—in July 1880—that Big Nose George was behind bars in Miles City, he made careful plans to bring the outlaw safely back to Rawlins for trial. He avoided traveling with his prisoner through the outlaw infested Powder River country and did not want to repeat the fiasco of Dutch Charley's train ride the year before. Instead, he chose an alternative route, longer and more circuitous, but less dangerous.

Much has been written about Rankin's travels to collect Big Nose George and return him to face justice in Carbon County. Three of the more comprehensive treatments are Meschter, Rankin, and Atwell.[39] These accounts do not agree on every detail, but suffice it to say the outlaw was taken east several hundred miles from Miles

City, then southward to Omaha where Rankin boarded the Union Pacific train with his prisoner. The only known photograph of Big Nose George, a studio portrait, probably was taken during their short stay in Omaha in the midst of his extradition. A print of this photo was presented by Mr. John C. Gale, System Chief, Special Agent in Omaha, presumably to the UPRR Museum.[40] Copies were widely circulated throughout Rawlins.

Parott and Rankin's journey by train from Omaha into Wyoming Territory became exciting in spite of the sheriff's precautions. The two men arrived in Laramie in early August. Sheriff Boswell kept an eye on the prisoner while Rankin oversaw the construction of a special train seat on which the outlaw could be manacled for the duration of the ride to Rawlins.[41] Then the Number Three train began the next leg of the journey, toward the coal mine community of Carbon, and then on to Rawlins.

When the train pulled into Carbon, the same town where Dutch Charley had been hanged over a year earlier, several armed masked men boarded the sheriff's car.[42] Rankin drew his revolver and held it on the intruders, refusing to turn over the prisoner. But the mob overpowered the authorities, broke Parott's irons, and put a rope around his neck. Then they hustled Parott outside to a corral where a high beam was attached across a couple of vertical poles. Standing at the end of the rope under the beam, Parott heard of the earlier fate of Dutch Charley in the same community. He said nervously, "I do not want to die with a lie in my mouth, and I will tell the truth, so help me God; but, give me a little time, I am so badly scared I can hardly talk."[43]

One of the men told him he could have all the time he needed. Big Nose George gave his name as George Francis Warden, then proceeded to tell the mob his side of the Elk Mountain murders. Parott admitted to being in the gang who killed Widdowfield and Vincent. He named Frank Tole, Mack (McKinney aka Frank James), Dutch Charley, Jack Campbell, Thomas Reed, Sim Wan, and himself as the outlaws who perpetrated the murders. For some reason, he did not mention John Wells (Sandy), though Wells undoubtedly was a gang member, but he may have left the group temporarily just before the murders.

Parott said that he only saw Joe Minuse five days after the crime when he was on the Green River, suggesting Parott and his partners took a circuitous route to the Powder River country after the Elk Mountain murders. Big Nose George may have related the Elk Mountain story to Minuse at this time, before Minuse and Dutch Charley spoke at Rock Creek.

Then Parott said he heard that Mack died of fever in the Yellowstone country, which is odd because Parott later would tell Leech that Mack was McKinney, an alias for Frank James who was still alive and at large. James's name and alias had been listed on the indictment since April 7, 1879. Perhaps, if one of the outlaws did die in the Yellowstone country, it may have been Tom Reed rather than Mack or some other accomplice.

After his half-hour confession, the mob put the prisoner back on the train as it pulled out of the station on its way to Rawlins. Everyone in Carbon attended a big dance following their slight intermission at the corral beam with Parott, satisfied authorities had the right man.

The jail register,[44] which is preserved today at the Carbon County Museum in Rawlins, lists an entry for the arrival of George Parott at the jail late on Saturday, August 7, 1880. He would spend the rest of his mortal life in confinement there, the only perpetrator of the Elk Mountain murders ever to stand trial for his misdeeds.

Chapter Four

The Territory of Wyoming v. George Parott

THE BUSTLING community of Rawlins has served as the political seat of Carbon County since its inception. Settled since 1868, the town was first named "Rawlins Spring," after General John A. Rawlins whose troops protected the Union Pacific Railroad crew during that time. The 1880 census listed 1,491 town residents, which comprised thirty-six percent of the total countywide population. In numerical contrast, over 467,800 head of cattle grazed the Territory's rich pastures, as did vast herds of sheep.[1] Citizens labored in ranching and a variety of other urban and rural trades, providing a safe and profitable lifestyle for themselves and their families.

Carbon County's geopolitical borders originally spanned a vast mountain and basin landscape extending the full length of Wyoming Territory, from south to north.[2] But by 1880, the county stretched north only to Pease County, soon to be renamed Johnson County. This new northern limit of Carbon County stopped southwest of the Pumpkin Buttes region, still giving the sheriff a tremendous domain over which to search out badmen and collect taxes. Nonetheless, most residents lived along the UPRR corridor where settlement and commerce thrived, leaving the vast territory to the north mostly as open range.

Rawlins began printing a fine county newspaper just months before authorities jailed Big Nose George, so contemporary documents during his confinement are much more easily obtained than those for the period of the murders two years previous. The *Carbon County Journal*, a Democrat-leaning weekly under the editorship of John Friend, supplemented a series of legal documents preserved in the

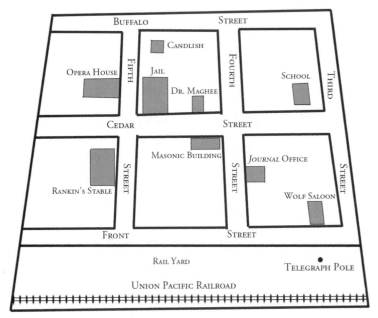

This map of Rawlins is from 1880–1885. Apparently Hugus took over the Fred Wolf property shortly after the Parott lynching. *Adapted from Meschter's book by author.*

district court files that provide researchers a comprehensive picture of what happened to the outlaw after his arrest.

The Big Nose George trial was the first real scoop covered from start to finish by the fledgling tabloid. Nothing like it had happened before in the small railroad community. The newspaper reported a flurry of legal activity throughout the fall and winter of 1880, convincing readers the Big Nose George case was a powerful test of Carbon County jurisprudence. The case also strained the solvency of the county treasury.

Demographic growth precipitated a need for adequate facilities to handle law enforcement requirements in Rawlins and the county. Courtroom space and new jail cells were a must. The first jail and courthouse was a wooden frame and log building on south Front Street, known as "The Alamo."[3] It was worn and aging after years of use, so a call went out in 1875 to build a new, stone facility.

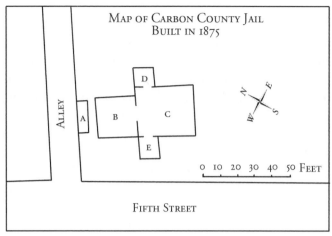

MAP OF CARBON COUNTY JAIL
BUILT IN 1875

ALLEY

A   B   C

D

E

FIFTH STREET

0 10 20 30 40 50 FEET

The single story, stone jailhouse was built in 1875. Only A and E were not stone. Rooms B, C, and D had a tin roof, while A and E were shingle. Room B would have easily held at least three cells, water closet, and corridor. Rooms C, D, and E may have served as offices, a cooking area, jailer space, and a parlor, but information is unclear as to where each function was performed in the jail. *Redrawn by author from specifications in Sanford Fire Insurance Map from Rawlins, Carbon County, Wyoming, 1883. Located at Library of Congress.*

County Clerk, P. L. Smith posted a request for proposals from the county commissioners for plans to build a one-story stone jail that included at least three cell units with a corridor, one large room, and at least three rooms for use by the jailer.[4] Specifications required a sheriff's office, a jailer room, and a cooking area. The largest room served as the parlor, a location used for small gatherings like the one prominently mentioned in the George Parott trial transcripts.

Architects completed this structure in September 1875 at a cost that did not exceed $4,500.[5] The facility sat on the northeast corner of Fifth and Cedar Streets in Rawlins, near the present location of the Ferguson building.[6] Bob Rankin, the undersheriff's brother, became jailer in the spring of 1878.[7] Bob's wife, Rosa, and their children moved into the new facility a year later when Rosa hired out as a cook for the inmates.

Unfortunately, the new jail did not provide any courtroom facilities, so the case against Big Nose George Parott would be heard in the

Masonic Building located on the southwest corner of Cedar and Fourth Streets, a block from the jail.[8] This two-story edifice was built in 1880, shortly before the Parott trial. County Commissioners entered into an agreement with the Masons to use the second floor as a courtroom during the fall term.[9] At the time of Parott's trial, the spacious interior also served as an opera and civic hall and provided space for various other public venues and private businesses. It filled to capacity with interested members of the community during Parott's trial. The actual Carbon County Courthouse itself would not be constructed until 1882, where the current Courthouse now stands.[10]

Authorities arraigned Parott on September 13, 1880, on the murder indictment describing the brutal death of Henry H. "Tip" Vincent. County Attorney, G.C. Smith, had hired well-known Cheyenne attorney, W.W. Corlett, to manage the prosecution at the arraignment. Corlett was a Civil War veteran and fervent Republican politician, who had served in territorial and national delegations. Just a year before, Corlett turned down the appointment of Chief Justice for the Territory of Wyoming, so he would have been familiar with the two associate justices, Blair and Peck, who both played a role in Parott's trial.[11] For some unknown reason, though, he never attended the murder trial after serving as prosecutor during Parott's arraignment.

Officials also hired Rawlins's own attorney, Homer Merrell, to assist Corlett in the prosecution. The court then appointed Samuel T. Lewis of Rawlins as defense counsel, to be assisted by C.W. Bramel of Laramie. Bramel proved to be a competent advocate, but Lewis suffered from alcoholism.[12]

Parott did not stand trial for the murder of Robert Widdowfield, nor did any other gang member. Prior statements already convinced county authorities that either Frank Tole or Dutch Charley had pulled the trigger on Widdowfield, and both of them were dead. That part of the Elk Mountain incident was closed.

Presiding judge at the arraignment, Jacob Blair, asked Parott of his guilt or innocence regarding the murder charge. Parott pled guilty. Blair described to Parott the severity of the charge and the

W.W. Corlett of Cheyenne, served as prosecuting attorney for Parott's arraignment. *Sub Neg 1686 (26709). Courtesy, Wyoming State Archives, Cheyenne, Wyoming.*

hanging sentence for those found guilty, wanting to assure himself that Parott understood the consequences of his plea. The prisoner knew at this point he was facing a charge that carried with it the death penalty.

Nonetheless, Parott reiterated, "I am guilty" and began to cry as he resumed his seat.[13] Attorney Corlett may have tangled the outlaw's thinking ahead of time, opening the door for the guilty plea, but history is silent on the circumstances behind Parott's response to Blair's inquiry.

Parott's attorneys should have talked with him prior to his plea and convinced him that a guilty plea would weaken or eliminate any defense they offered. Apparently, neither Lewis nor Bramel had advised the prisoner to enter a "not guilty" plea in front of the judge.

The courtroom sat stunned by the unanticipated spectacle of a prisoner pleading guilty to first degree murder. Loud murmurs echoed throughout the chamber, and gasps emanated from the audience. Yet, in spite of Parott's plea, Judge Blair still needed to hear some evidence. He instructed the prosecution to produce proof that Vincent and Widdowfield had indeed been murdered before he would pass sentence on Parott.

The courtroom cleared for the day. Ex-Union Pacific detective, M.F. Leech, now a northern Colorado businessman who had come to town for the arraignment, walked over to the jail with Undersheriff James Rankin. He asked permission to visit with the accused man during the recess. After all, Parott had pled guilty, so there should be no problem posing a few questions. Leech, obsessed by the Elk Mountain murders, hoped to draw details out of the prisoner.

Rankin and Leech walked with Dr. Maghee, the local physician, over to the sheriff's parlor, where they sat with the prisoner. Two other unnamed men joined them there. Then an extensive conversation with Parott followed; Leech asking pointed questions and the outlaw answering them. Defense attorneys Lewis and Bramel apparently had not been invited and had yet to warn Parott to keep his mouth shut.

Parott spoke with his attorneys only after the parlor conversation. They gave him second thoughts about declaring his guilt. He wisely changed his plea to not guilty on Friday afternoon, September 17, but the parlor chat already had damaged the defense's case.

Judge Blair had intended to come to Rawlins on September 25 to pass sentence on Parott, but when the inmate pled not guilty, it rendered an immediate sentence illegal.[14] A sentence could not be handed down when court was not in session.[15] The suspect's new plea required a jury trial, so court adjourned until November 8, giving all concerned parties time to prepare their case.

Then the outlaw changed his plea to guilty once again, throwing the court's plans into total confusion. Parott requested that Blair be telegraphed, asking him to come to Rawlins to hand down a sentence, preferring to die at the hands of the law, rather than from the violence of a mob.[16] The plea of not guilty must have angered some Rawlins residents, and the prisoner sensed strong animosity growing against him. His mental anxiety was palpable, but the plea reversal did not affect the court's docket at all. The murder trial was still scheduled for November.

Meanwhile, the Democratic ticket for the office of Carbon County Sheriff was filed by October 16, 1880,[17] listing Isaac C. Miller of Rawlins as their candidate. His Republican opponent would be James G. Rankin, the undersheriff who recently brought Big Nose George in from Montana. November 2 was election day, Miller won the sheriff's seat, beating Rankin with a forty-three-vote majority, 693 to 650.[18] Parott sat in jail while the voting took place. Miller may have helped prepare a panel of prospective jurors to be interviewed for petit jury selection in the upcoming criminal murder case.

By Monday, November 8, George Parott was convinced that Judge Blair was biased against him in trial preparations, so he signed an affidavit requesting a change of venue.[19] Parott penned his signature on the document using the single "r", two "t" version of his last name, which is the version used throughout this book.

One wonders why Parott only complained against Judge Blair in the affidavit yet had no objection against Judge Peck as a replacement. William Ware Peck, an associate justice of the Wyoming Supreme Court along with Blair, was known for incurring enormous court expenses, among other traits.[20]

Instead, Parott should have requested a trial transfer to an entirely different judicial district where the local populace was less hostile and where he may have been able to save his life. His legal defense team erred in not prompting such a request.

Parott's change of venue complaint placed Peck as presiding judge. Attorneys Bramel and Lewis remained the defense counsel, while Corlett, Merrell, and Smith would conduct the prosecution.[21] Merrell eventually withdrew his participation, temporarily, but eventually returned to lead the prosecution.

The trial of Big Nose George Parott for the murder of Henry H. Vincent convened on Tuesday, November 16, 1880, at eleven o'clock in the morning.[22] Court assistants brought in extra chairs to seat the growing number of interested spectators who came to the Masonic Building to hear testimony. This became one of the biggest social events of the year in the small town.

The first order of business was jury selection and swearing in those citizens chosen to deliberate. The twelve men selected for jury duty were Thomas Creighton, George Birmingham, A.W. Reynolds, Walter French, W.W. Chapman, E.L. Swazey, O.A. Hamilton, A.W. Eaton, E.J. Bowen, Charles Kesterton, L.W. Kling, and C.E. Rand.

Allowing for possible confusion caused by spelling variations, some of these men can be tentatively identified. At least a few were stockmen and county businessmen. Bowen was a hotel proprietor from Fort Steele. W.W. Chapman apparently was an early pioneer who had written a short diary of his trip through the Sweetwater country in 1849-1850, long before Rawlins was settled.[23] Unfolding events in Parott's trial would preclude the need for any of these men to deliberate on a vote of guilt or innocence.

The life of Big Nose George depended on a favorable trial outcome. It did not matter whether he pulled the trigger sending a fatal bullet into Henry Vincent or not. The prosecution needed only to prove beyond a reasonable doubt that he had been a direct accomplice in the crime committed near Elk Mountain.

As author Muehlberger stated in his discussion of the trial of Frank James for a separate murder, "Under the felony murder rule then and now, if someone is killed during the commission of a felony, all participants are guilty of the murder, regardless of who pulled the trigger."[24] Parott already had admitted in front of Leech and other witnesses at the parlor to having been in the gang at Elk Mountain, but later insisted he was not guilty of murder.

Deliberations immediately became contentious when prosecutor Smith requested a continuance until his colleague, Mr. Corlett, could attend. But Corlett never appeared again after the arraignment. Perhaps he felt he had done his job when Parott gave his initial guilty plea.

The defense opposed any delay and objected to Smith's motion. The prosecution eventually complied, later making a statement about the evidence they planned to present. Proceedings adjourned until Wednesday, November 17.[25]

Trial attendees on Wednesday morning heard court discussions over minor issues of law and dilatory motions presented by Smith. Merrell then returned to lead Parott's criminal prosecution. Homer Merrell was a well-known attorney in the community and quite capable of effective courtroom examination. His precise questioning would build an iron-clad case against the outlaw.

Thirteen potential prosecution witnesses were subpoenaed to appear in court and be prepared to testify,[26] but only six were sworn in. Four of those not sworn included Dr. Maghee who had been present during the parlor discussion with Parott and could confirm that Dutch Charley was one of the guilty parties. Joseph Widdowfield, Robert's brother,[27] was not called probably because the case didn't address Parott's role in Widdowfield's murder. Ed Dickinson was absent due to an inspection of a Union Pacific train accident, and J.C. Friend, editor of the *Carbon County Journal*, who only needed to give the court a copy of his newspaper's coverage of Parott's interview in the months before the court date.

The final three men subpoenaed but not called were James Bellamy, William McCarty, and W.S. Cox. Two of these men may have been the "anonymous" witnesses to Parott's parlor discussion with Leech.

The court swore in each prosecution witness separately. Merrell and Smith then needed to compile evidence that two murders indeed had been committed along Rattlesnake Creek, that lawmen Widdowfield and Vincent were killed there by several gunshots, and that their bodies were later found by an organized posse. Such details would fulfill the parameters established by Judge Blair during Parott's arraignment on September 13.

Prosecutor Merrell called six witnesses to testify. In order of appearance, these were Undersheriff James G. Rankin, John F. Foote, William Daley, Jesse Wallace, Taylor Pennock, and M.F. Leech. The first five were well-known Carbon County residents familiar with the murdered lawmen, and most had ridden with the posse.

The final witness was M.F. Leech, former UPRR detective, who came to Rawlins to relate the facts of Parott's parlor conversation.

Leech had registered for a room at the Maxwell House (the old Railroad Hotel) on November 15, and stayed for the trial. [28] Merrell figured this witness would be his coup de grâce.

When called to the stand, Rankin told of the telegram he received while riding the Number Three train to Rawlins on August 17, the subsequent tracking effort, and concluded when the posse found the bodies of Widdowfield and Vincent lying about fifty yards apart. He did not clearly see the body of his friend Henry Vincent because he had been reluctant to look too closely.[29] Neither Lewis nor Bramel offered any cross-examination according to court proceedings. Lewis made objections that Peck overruled during testimony.

John F. Foote testified that he owned the ranch at the base of Elk Mountain, which had been circumvented by the outlaws' trail on August 18. He knew Vincent and was present when his body was found lying squarely on its back and covered in brush near the head of Rattlesnake Creek. Foote pointed to a place on his breast where Vincent had been shot and added there were two other wounds in his leg.

Judge Peck clarified a few questions and answers with direct inquiries himself. Then the defense established that Vincent's body had swollen some but not decayed much. The body was not far from the horse trail followed by the two lawmen when they tracked the gang.

Merrell elicited testimony of the campfire and the discovery of a gun and old saddle about seventy-five yards to the east. Unfortunately, witnesses gave dramatically different estimates of the distance between the two bodies, varying up to two hundred yards. If anyone took deliberate measurements to define the space between the two dead men, those records have not been found.

Lewis questioned Foote, establishing that many people camped overnight while riding the trail, so campfires often burned in the country. The court then heard that Vincent's body was subsequently brought back to Rawlins and buried.

William Daley testified he had been a Rawlins resident since 1869. He was in the party that discovered the two bodies, and when he examined Vincent, he noticed a large wound on the right breast beneath the lawman's blue shirt. A forty-five or fifty caliber bullet entered the torso from the back and exited out the front, making a larger wound.

Merrell then asked Daley to, "State if you noticed any other marks."[30]

Daley responded that two smaller wounds were inflicted from the front, one lower down on the right chest and one higher up. John Foote already had testified about two gunshot wounds in one of Vincent's legs and the large chest wound. Bill Daley established that the chest wound initiated in Vincent's back and exited in his front, then added that he saw two other smaller chest wounds. These witnesses described a total of five wounds in the body of Henry Vincent.

Vincent's feet were bare, his boots having been taken, and his hat was absent as well. Daley described an old cartridge belt fastened around the deceased's right leg near the knee. The outlaws had dragged the body into the timber, then placed pine boughs over it. Daley also found the Springfield carbine abandoned near one of the campfires and kept it in his possession.

His testimony placed Widdowfield's body two hundred yards away from Vincent's, a much greater interval than described by Rankin. If such a space existed between the two bodies, one might assume that Vincent rode quite a distance up the canyon to escape the outlaws' gunfire, and the outlaws had to run on foot to keep him within revolver range. Either that or the bodies were moved farther apart after they were killed.

It is more conceivable that Vincent was killed within fifty yards of the outlaws' camp where handguns were much more effective. These smaller caliber weapons seemingly generated the other wounds which entered the chest from the front.

Widdowfield's body was in a more putrid state than Vincent's, according to Daley, and exhibited a single gunshot wound that entered near the man's eye before exiting out the side of his head and neck. Widdowfield had been easy to identify because of familiar objects of clothing still on his person.[31] The line of questioning related to Widdowfield's murder prompted a rapid response from defense counsel.

Lewis moved to strike Daley's testimony regarding Widdowfield's body, which Judge Peck granted. The defendant was not on trial for the murder of Robert Widdowfield, so related testimony was irrelevant. Merrell had to focus only on establishing Parott's guilt in the murder of Tip Vincent.

Jesse Wallace, the fourth prosecution witness, had lived in Rawlins for about eight years. He also was a good friend of Tip Vincent's and knew him well. He testified that several bullet holes occurred on both sides of Vincent's exposed breast, some entry wounds and at least one exit wound, confirming earlier testimony. Wallace said the bodies were found on August 27, 1878, then noted that old stirrup straps and saddle girths had been cut off and discarded at the campsite. The outlaws must have geared up before leaving the camp after the two homicides.

Wallace mentioned the land surveyor whom the posse met near Rattlesnake Canyon and who took them part way up the creek toward where he had heard several gunshots on August 19. Under Lewis's cross-examination, Wallace testified that he not only had seen the wounds in Vincent's breast, but also the corresponding holes in the blue shirt Vincent was wearing after Daley had pulled it away to examine the corpse.

Taylor Pennock, a resident of Warm Springs, reiterated much of what already had been established, then testified he had been in the party that took Vincent's body from the murder scene to Fort Steele, for transport to Rawlins.

The first part of Merrell's prosecution case concluded. He had meticulously established the evidence Judge Blair requested at arraignment. The jury understood the who, what, where, when, and how of the Elk Mountain incident. Merrell must now expose Parott's role in the murders, and he planned to take full advantage of the parlor conversation to do so. His questioning of Leech would hammer the final nail into Parott's coffin.

But phase two of the prosecution proved much more contentious than the first, with damning direct examination, futile cross-examination, and a spattering of pointed objections amid strong rebuttals. Merrell centered on the conversation between Leech and Parott in the sheriff's parlor, in which the accused voluntarily participated without any coercion or enticement.

Lewis had to fight this line of questioning if he and Bramel had any hope of saving their client from a noose. But Merrell treated Parott's parlor statements as a confession of guilt, and Lewis could not easily counter the argument because Parott already had admitted guilt during arraignment in front of Judge Blair before any conversation with Leech.

Leech retold the parlor conversation, admitting that Rankin had attended only part of the time. Dr. Thomas Maghee had been there only to convince himself that Dutch Charley was party to the Widdowfield and Vincent murders and had not been hanged unjustly. The two other men present, whom Leech claimed not to know, apparently were there for the entire dialogue.

Leech never identified either unnamed man, and we do not know if either was a prosecuting or defense attorney. It is clear, though, the outlaw had no legal counsel present and was not under oath at the time.

The two men whose names are not known never were called to testify in court, either to confirm or rebut Leech's testimony. Leech never pointed them out at trial, and neither signed affidavits or gave sworn testimony. Only Leech's personal recollections were entered into the record, so the entire parlor conversation would be characterized as hearsay in today's legal parlance.

In spite of all this, Homer Merrell asked Leech to begin his testimony by identifying himself and describing the structure of the parlor conversation.[32] Lewis quickly objected to any testimony referring to the parlor conversation, at which time Judge Peck asked his own questions of the witness. Defense renewed their objection twice, but questioning by the court proceeded.

Leech explained he had asked Rankin to allow the interview because there were some points related to the crime that Parott could clarify since he had admitted to being present when the two law enforcement officers were killed. Leech testified Parott had not been coerced to speak, but was glad to have the opportunity to talk. Had one of the two "anonymous" listeners been a defense attorney, it is almost certain legal counsel would have intervened at this point.

Merrell intended to prove the parlor conversation constituted an oral confession by Parott to the murder of Vincent, given willingly to Leech in the presence of four witnesses. Lewis vehemently objected to the tactic, stating that the preliminary examination made of Parott to the court had shown that any alleged testimony by the accused was incompetent. After all, Parott had changed his plea at least twice in an irrational flurry of indecision.

Judge Peck overruled the defense's objection, and Lewis took exception. Parott's parlor statements were now free to be accepted as evidence in court and, true or false, they would lead Big Nose George to the gallows.

Leech then stated he had asked Parott about the train derailment near Como, the murders of the two lawmen, and any culpability of Joe Minuse.

Parott had whimpered, "Ever since that murder, every time I shut my eyes nearly, I see those men, and anything that I can do to bring the balance of them to justice, I will be glad to do it."[33]

Parott told Leech the story of the gang gathering in Powder River country, naming each of the outlaws and their aliases, and their ride together to Medicine Bow. Parott remembered the gang intended to rob the eastbound train, but the engine almost knocked him off the trestle when it rushed by. He added their leader, McKinney, was an alias of Frank James. The gang retreated to Elk Mountain after the train incident, arriving there Sunday afternoon. On Monday morning the guard at the wickiup first saw two riders heading toward the canyon.

Parott identified Frank Tole as the man who shot Widdowfield in the face, killing him instantly. The rest of the gang opened up on Vincent who was still horseback. Joe Minuse had ridden to Brown's Park before this crime unfolded and was not back in Wyoming until after it was all over. Parott admitted Minuse did not participate.

After the murders, Parott rode with some other outlaws up north to the Goose Creek country where they split up. He pondered that he might return to Utah where he once worked as a teamster for the Central Pacific railroad and told Leech he now regretted not doing so.

Lewis attempted to pull details out of Leech's discussion with the outlaw. He tried to establish that Leech was still a detective for the railroad, perhaps implying entrapment, but Merrell objected. Lewis then unsuccessfully continued to object to the court allowing any testimony related to the parlor conversation. Meschter, in his book, pointed out Lewis's exception to Peck's ruling and added that Lewis should have used it later as a foundation for appeal, but did not do so.[34] This oversight did not bode well for the accused outlaw.

Lewis cross-examined Leech further, but the witness could not recall if Parott had said how he came to join the outlaw gang or whether he had been working on a ranch and was coerced into it. Leech also could not recall whether Parott had told him he had been compelled by threats and intimidation to join the gang in the first place. At least, Parott's attorneys were finally looking for a way to mitigate the negative impact of the parlor conversation.

The court discovered that Parott had warned McKinney (Frank James) not to shoot the section man at Como, stating he would have to shoot Parott first, which argues that the accused had some empathy for the innocent. Lewis attempted unsuccessfully to get Leech to state that McKinney (James) called Parott a coward at the trestle, at which time the bad blood in the gang developed. He did recall, however, that Frank Tole left the party after bad blood boiled over near Elk Mountain, and Tole later told Joe Minuse the argument was his reason for leaving. If this actually was the sequence of events, it might place Frank Tole as passing through the Rock Creek country, where he met Minuse on his way to the Black Hills.

Merrell closed prosecution arguments and rested his case. Now the defense needed to inject reasonable doubt into the jury and try to destroy the impact of the parlor discussion.

The whole parlor conversation smacks of unconfirmed reporting. The efficacy of Parott's "confession" is suspect for many reasons. It seems inconceivable that a man would be sentenced to death on such a vague standard of evidence in this modern era, without warning the defendant that anything he said could be used against him in court. But Parott's case was decided long before the important

William Ware Peck was an associate justice of the Wyoming Supreme Court. *Courtesy, Wyoming State Archives, Cheyenne, Wyoming.*

Supreme Court Miranda decision. No wonder Lewis vigorously attacked the parlor conversation.

Thursday, November 18, was Lewis's opportunity to present the defense, but he never got a chance to call witnesses, and the accused never testified under oath at any time. Instead, Parott—knowing full well the potential consequence of any statement he might make—entered a guilty plea once again. Judge Peck ordered the murder indictment to be read aloud, then asked Parott once more how he pled. Parott spoke in a faltering voice… "guilty."[35] Peck discharged the petit jury, who would not have to deliberate on a verdict.

Bramel, the optimistic defense attorney, holding out hope for a prison sentence instead of the gallows, warned Parott that pleading guilty to the indictment might be interpreted as guilt to murder either in the first or second degree. Second degree murder was an offense without deliberation or premeditation.[36] While the indictment against Parott did not specify the degree of murder, it did state that Parott "...deliberately, premeditatedly, and of his malice afore-thought"[37] shot and killed Henry H. Vincent. Thus, the indictment clearly focused on an extreme case of murder subject to the death penalty. Deliberation and premeditation were later listed as preconditions in the definition of first-degree murder when the 1884 statute was written.[38]

Lewis and Bramel, and a number of authorities, still believed the plea entered by Parott was only for second degree murder.[39] They argued that evening regarding their understanding of the charge, so a recess was taken until 8:00 P.M., at which time Lewis moved for a suspension of sentencing. Judge Peck took it under advisement.

The case against Parott would not conclude until noon on December 15, 1880. This delay gave Parott nearly a month to ponder his fate before sentencing. There was little left to do in his defense. His guilty plea pre-empted any appeal on Lewis's part. Legal maneuvering now focused only on the suspension of sentencing.

The courtroom filled to capacity on Wednesday, December 15, with curious spectators milling about. Officers of the district court shuffled important papers, as the scheduled hearing neared. High drama permeated the Rawlins community; a man's life depended on the outcome of a trial held in the room where the community attended operas. But the performance today was real. Judge Peck arrived ten minutes early and waited fully until noon to pass sentence, already having visited George Parott in his jail cell to render some fatherly advice.[40]

Peck offered to let ex-Governor John Thayer sit to his right hand for the proceedings. Then he addressed Lewis's motion for arrest of judgment filed on November 18, claiming the Grand Jury, which found the murder indictment as true under signature of Foreman J.F. Crawford, was not legally constituted. Lewis had added that the facts of the case did not represent an offense punishable by death, and the indictment itself was vague and indefinite, therefore not fully informing the defendant of the crime with which he was charged.[41]

In addition to the question of degree of murder, the vagueness may be explained by the fact that several different indictments existed on file, and each one named a different outlaw as the man who killed Vincent. But Lewis's motion served only as a brief delaying tactic.

At 12:25 P.M. on December 15, Judge Peck overruled Lewis's motion. The judge treated M.F. Leech's testimony as a Parott confession, as if it came from the lips of the defendant himself. There followed opposition to the motion for sentencing on the grounds that the indictment charged only second-degree murder, but the judge held the argument to be meritless, and continued to sentencing.

Peck ordered Big Nose George Parott to stand in front of the bench and asked him if he had anything to say about why the sentence should not be passed upon him. Parott replied, "I have not, your honor."

Parott sat down to listen to a brief summary of the case. He originally pled guilty from a conviction of his conscience, then changed his plea to not guilty, which prompted the trial, and at the end changed his plea back to guilty. The court waited half a day to accept the final plea in case the accused might change his mind once again.

Judge Peck offered, as an act of compassion, that Parott should "disabuse your mind of any idea that there is any shadow of a chance that the sentence of the law will not be carried into effect, or that there will be any postponement."[42] The same edition of the *Carbon County Journal* quoted Peck as saying the "sentence of the Court will be strictly carried out, and although there can be no mercy expected from the earthly judge, you may seek and obtain mercy and pardon from the Heavenly Judge, before whom you are soon to appear, and although you have led a life of crime, may you die a Christian man."

District Court transcripts contain Peck's decision that stated George Parott had "been duly convicted in this Court, by his plea of 'Guilty' of the crime of murder in the 'First Degree.'"[43] In the end, Parott's own words had convicted him of a hanging offense.

No response from Parott was recorded. Peck had him stand once more. The convicted prisoner was supported on his right by defense counsel Sam T. Lewis and on his left by Sheriff Rankin. Judge Peck ordered all in the room to rise while he rendered sentence. The entire crowd stood, eyes riveted on the judge and the guilty man, mesmerized by the unfolding legal spectacle:

"[The] sentence of the Court is, that you, George Parrot, on the second day of April, in the year of our Lord 1881, between the hours of ten o'clock in the forenoon and four o'clock in the afternoon, in the place and manner prescribed by law, in the County of Carbon and Territory of Wyoming, and by proper officers be hanged by the neck until you are dead."[44]

The judge ordered a transcript of the testimony be made by the stenographer and filed by the Clerk of the Court, to be paid for by the County Treasurer.[45] J.C.F. Richardson, the official Stenographer of Wyoming Territory, signed and certified the transcripts on March 18, 1881. Presiding Judge William Ware Peck certified the same on April 4, 1881. G.C. Smith, Prosecuting Attorney, certified the document as well. Attorney C.W. Bramel was paid fifty dollars for defending Big Nose George during the trial.[46] Parott's life would end in the midst of these administrative deliberations.

Big Nose George wept violently throughout the final court proceedings and required assistance in leaving the courtroom after Peck pronounced his sentence.[47] The former outlaw now had plenty of time to sit in his cell and ponder the fate of those who transgress the law. That got him to thinking.

Undersheriff James Rankin brought Big Nose George to Rawlins for trial. *Courtesy, Carbon County Museum, Rawlins, Wyoming.*

Ike Miller was Sheriff of Carbon County from 1880–1884. This photograph is circa 1899. *Courtesy, Carbon County Museum, Rawlins, Wyoming.*

Chapter Five

Ligature Asphyxia

SHERIFF MILLER posted notices to all parties once he took office in January 1881, warning them that he would strictly enforce the law against carrying concealed weapons in Rawlins. The *Carbon County Journal* noted the "festive shootist better look a little out, or he will come to grief as Ike is one of that sort of men who will stand no foolishness."[1] Miller already had made several arrests of people violating the concealed weapon law by the first week of January.

Clearly, some members of the community already showed growing agitation regarding the presence of a jailed prisoner who had confessed to murdering one of Rawlins's own lawmen. Parott became dismayed from the murmurings around town and worried he might not survive until his scheduled date of execution. But by early February, his spirits had somewhat recovered.[2]

William T. Schmalsle and William H. Irvine, both from Montana, each received $1,000 from the Carbon County Court general fund as a reward for their role in assisting in the arrest and conviction of Big Nose George Parott.[3] Matching funds were expected for each of them from the Union Pacific Railroad.

These were the first rewards paid out since the arrest of Dutch Charley in Green River back in 1879. When Boone May learned about the reward posted for the named murderers, he returned to the scene where he shot Frank Tole along the Black Hills stage route, found where the outlaw was buried, cut off his head, and took it to authorities to claim his own payment. However, Tole had never been arrested or convicted for the Elk Mountain murders. In fact, no authority yet knew about his involvement in the Carbon County crime at the time of his death, so May's reward request was denied.[4] Tole would not be the only member of the Powder River Gang with a grisly afterlife.

The county newspaper in January published census data for Rawlins and the region.[5] Carbon County listed a total population of 3,438, with 2,423 of this number being male and 1,015 female. Some 2,513 were native born, while 925 were listed as foreign. Whites (Caucasians) represented over ninety-eight percent of the population at 3,392, while "Colored" was only 1.4 percent at 46 residents. Carbon County's ethnic and cultural diversity was just beginning to develop, and people were coming from several states and other countries to live there. Among these residents were citizens who would witness George Parott's last days on earth.

A man who would figure prominently in the Big Nose George story arrived in Rawlins from Bristol, Vermont, on Thursday morning, February 17.[6] Dr. John Osborne, a future Governor of Wyoming, came to the community and entered medical practice with the well-known Dr. Thomas Maghee. Maghee was the Union Pacific surgeon and Rawlins physician who had witnessed part of Parott's parlor confession.[7] The two medical professionals maintained an office on the northwest corner of the intersection of Fourth and Cedar Streets, on the opposite end of the block and down Cedar Street from the jail.

By March 5, Parott had grown increasingly nervous and morose regarding his anticipated fate, according to Jailer Bob Rankin, who observed him daily. Big Nose George had almost lost his appetite and often was sleepless the closer he got to his execution date. Authorities soon administered him chloral to induce sleep and help him relax.[8] Parott's anxiety had been profound before the drugging, and therefore required the treatment.

Community discourse on street corners and in shops focused more and more on Parott's upcoming execution. Many residents wanted to witness the convict's legal hanging, a desire that prompted Sheriff Miller to publish in the newspaper Sections 170 and 173 of the compiled laws of Wyoming relating to executions:

This two-story Masonic Building was where Parott's trial was held. Circa 1880. *Courtesy, Carbon County Museum, Rawlins, Wyoming.*

"Section 170. When any person shall be sentenced to be hung, such punishment shall be inflicted in the immediate vicinity of the jail, within an inclosure to be prepared for that purpose under the direction of the sheriff, which inclosure shall be higher than the gallows and so constructed as to exclude the view of persons outside thereof."

"Section 173. Besides the sheriff and his assistants, the following persons may be present at the execution and none others: The clergyman in attendance upon the prisoner, such other persons as the prisoner may designate, not exceeding six in number, and such other persons as the sheriff may designate, not exceeding twelve in number."

He reminded the *Carbon County Journal* it was his full intention to carry out the law exactly as written and declared that all persons should govern themselves accordingly.[9]

Sheriff Miller did not want any passersby to observe the execution if they had not been invited to attend. The legal hanging of Big Nose George would be a closed, private affair with no public gawking allowed. This ruling probably frustrated many townsfolk who had been close friends with Widdowfield and Vincent and were anxious to see at least one of the murderers pay for his ruthless crime. Even though citizens wanted to witness the legal hanging, Sheriff Miller planned to carry out the letter of the law.[10]

On Saturday, March 19, 1881, the *Carbon County Journal* announced that in two weeks Big Nose George would "climb the golden stair" via the hempen line.[11] The Reverend Dr. Claxton of Cheyenne visited the prisoner in jail to provide spiritual comfort. Claxton speculated that the outlaw was likely to become a Christian before the scheduled execution date.

Meanwhile, two county residents also appeared in the paper about this time, under rather innocuous circumstances. B.T. Ryan was offering twelve thoroughbred Shorthorn bulls at seventy-five dollars each in a newspaper notice. In another story, Charles Mc-Carien was placed in charge of the lemonade stand at a community social event. Both of these men would soon reappear in reference to the Big Nose George story.

Then, during the week of March 19–26, Sheriff Ike Miller visited the Sand Creek country out near the eastern end of the Ferris Mountains, possibly to collect taxes from the residents or perform other law enforcement duties. The railroad town of Rawlins and surrounding area settled into its daily routine in spite of the pending execution.

—•—

Tuesday, March 22, 1881, is a date forever etched into Rawlins history as one of its most turbulent and darkest days. The early part of the day was ordinary, but events later on unfolded in chaotic succession, and they reverberate to this day.

Big Nose George was busy in his cell that afternoon, after somehow getting his hands on a boy's single bladed knife two-and-a-half inches long with a hawk bill point.[12] He also had managed to conceal a small sandstone rock he used as a makeshift whetstone. All afternoon he ground the blade back and forth along the stone, painstakingly sharpening the edge so he could saw through the rivets that blacksmith James Candlish had used to pin the shackles around the outlaw's ankles.

Parott freed himself from the chains, then hid in a nearby water closet until about 7:30 P.M. when an opportunity presented itself to get the drop on jailer Bob Rankin. Prisoners typically were allowed to move along the corridor out of their cells during the day, which was separated from the jailer's room by a locked door. Jailer Rankin soon entered the corridor to put prisoners inside their cells and lock each door and the corridor for the night.

Parott picked the perfect moment when the jailer's back was turned, then swung the heavy shackles hard against Rankin's head, repeating the process two more times and opening ugly head wounds that oozed blood. The jailer hollered for his wife, who lived in the building with him, to quick bring his pistol. Parott stepped back after assaulting the jailer, turned his head slightly away, and Rankin hit him in the side of the neck with his fist. The blow knocked Parott against the corridor wall, giving Rankin time to stumble out the door that separated the corridor from the jailer's room.

Rosa Rankin heard the commotion from her vantage point in the parlor area and then heard Rankin's scream for his pistol. She came in and rushed over to close and lock the grated door into the corridor after Rankin exited through it and while Parott was still inside. Once the jailer was safely outside the corridor, Parott crept back into the water closet, no longer able to make it outdoors to steal a horse for his planned getaway. One of the other prisoners was ordered to light a lamp in the corridor, exposing Parott's hideaway, so the outlaw returned to his cell.

In an interesting coincidence, one of the other inmates was James Averell, in custody for a murder investigation in Buffalo. Averell would be released from jail some weeks later and settle in the Sweetwater country beyond Sand Creek. While living there in a roadhouse, he would be grabbed by a vigilante group eight years later in 1889 and lynched along with Ella Watson (Cattle Kate) for alleged cattle thievery.[13]

The whole affair with Parott in the county jail caused immediate concern among the citizens of Rawlins, and primal rage escalated against the convicted outlaw. A crowd began to gather around the jail.

Rosa Rankin was the wife of the jailer, Bob Rankin. *Courtesy, Carbon County Museum, Rawlins, Wyoming*

Parott was ordered to come out of his cell and sit on a bench in the corridor where he apologized to Rankin for hitting him so hard. Then the authorities found the sharpened knife and worn piece of sandstone in his cell. New rivets were quickly fashioned and the shackles put back on the prisoner. Everything quieted down for a while, but small groups of men still gathered in hushed dialogue out on the street, unwilling to let just anyone in on their conversations.

Rumors circulated among the populace that Big Nose George was to be broken out of jail and lynched by irate citizens of the railroad community before his legally scheduled execution. Several groups of two or three men walked toward the jail about 10:00 P.M. after their street conversations abated. The injured jailer was still recuperating on a lounge in his room when a guard named Simms heard a rap at the door and a voice demanding admittance.[14]

When Simms asked the visitor to identify himself, he heard the simple answer, "Friends." Simms argued that it was too late for any visit. He was the lone guard on duty at the jail as his partner, Landon, already had gone to get a gun, anticipating trouble.

Then the jailhouse door burst open and several pistols were aimed at the guard. Entry happened so quickly all Simms could do was drop his shotgun and put up his hands. One of the men entered Rankin's lounge room and held a gun on the injured jailer while another man removed the cell keys from his pocket. The vigilantes brought an axe to break into Parott's cell door if necessary to grab the prisoner.

Meanwhile, special guard John Landon was returning to the jail from his short errand when one of the vigilantes met him in the yard. The masked man told Landon it would be best for him to take a walk, and the request was backed up with a drawn pistol. Vigilantes in the jail manhandled the confessed murderer to herd him outside toward the southeast part of town. The entire affair was quiet, quick, and covert so that very few citizens knew anything about it until it was almost over. It was nearing 11:00 P.M., and many residents already were in bed.

When newspaper representatives heard of the incident in progress, they rushed to the scene of commotion down the street and noticed about a hundred quiet, well-behaved bystanders milling about. The *Carbon County Journal* reported that, "[the] lookers-on being among some of the best people of the town tax-payers and law-abiding citizens, … all seemed to be fully satisfied with the lynching of the prisoner, while at the same time condemning the apparent necessity requiring such a proceeding."[15] The contrasting tension between right and wrong emerged in the behavior of the gathering throng, but peer pressure exerted among several masked men guided community revenge and ruled the day.

This photograph of Front Street in Rawlins was taken within a year or two of the lynching. *Courtesy, Carbon County Museum, Rawlins, Wyoming.*

Some of the lynching activity had taken place before the newspaper men arrived. The vigilantes took Parott to a telegraph pole in front of Fred Wolf's saloon as the curious crowd gathered. Every actual participant in the lynching was masked. One of them brought a rope and fastened it up the telegraph pole, while another brought in a large barrel a few feet tall.

A third man, in a white mask, placed the rope around Parott's neck while the outlaw stood on the barrel, then the masked man said "All right."[16] There is no mention whether or not the rope had been previously tied into a hangman's noose, so it may simply have had the typical honda knot standard on any lasso. No preparation had been made to ensure the outlaw would break his neck from a calculated drop distance, which would have hastened his death and been more humane.

One of the masked men hollered, "'Kick the barrel,' and it was done."[17] Unfortunately, Parott fell clear to the ground. The rope may have slipped down the telegraph pole if there was no cross-beam on which to loop it. And no rope length measurements had been taken to ensure a successful drop and quick execution. Another man hollered, "Hang him over and make a good job of it this time."[18]

The newspaper reporter arrived at the scene just as someone brought a ladder and placed it against the telegraph pole. Two masked men helped Parott climb the ladder until he scaled the rungs for about seven or eight feet. This time, the vigilante in the white mask adjusted the rope to a more suitable length.

Parott stood on a ladder rung and pleaded to the crowd, "It is a shame to take a man's life this way. Give me time and I will climb the ladder myself, and when I get high enough, I will jump off."[19] But someone pulled the ladder out from under the condemned man and his hands came untied. He grasped around the telegraph pole trying to prevent the rope tension from tightening around his neck.

He gripped the pole, pulled himself up seven or eight feet, and pleaded once again with the crowd, "For God sake, someone shoot me, do not let me choke to death!"[20] Nobody responded to the man's frantic plea. The outlaw slid down the pole and climbed back up a couple of times before he wore out. Eventually his arms slid to his sides while he dangled there, choking to death at the end of the rope. The crowd had nearly doubled by this time.

Someone tapped S.T. Lewis (the outlaw's attorney) on the shoulder and said, "Doctor, see if that man is dead yet."[21] Lewis felt for the man's pulse and pronounced him dead. A doctor in the crowd, probably Osborne, also felt the pulse but said the outlaw was still alive, so they left him hanging.

The suffocated outlaw was dead by midnight, and the coroner ordered William Daley to cut the body down from the telegraph pole as the crowd dispersed. The townspeople who had wanted to witness the quick legal hanging of Parott instead had the unenviable opportunity of watching him die a slow, strangulation death at the hands of vigilantes.

A man named Thomas Rooney sketched the Big Nose George lynching from an eyewitness description of the event, and the drawing is now on file in the Wyoming Department of State Parks and Cultural Resources, State Archives, and State Museum.[22] The scene depicts a telegraph pole about six feet north of the railroad tracks and across Front Street from the town buildings. Big Nose George dangles from a stretched rope around his neck, with shackles on his ankles and one arm loosely gripping the pole. A sack covers his head. Groups of onlookers stand nearby next to their horses, but none of the men seem to be wearing a mask. One horse in the lower left of the drawing stands behind a group of bystanders and may provide a clue to the event.

The left hip of the horse shows a Two-Bar S brand (an equal sign above a capital S). A state brand inspector looked at the sketch and checked the brand records for Wyoming, but he could not find such a horse brand in any of the registrations he reviewed.[23] The horse may have belonged to a nonresident who happened to be in Rawlins that evening and observed the lynching. Frankly, it could just be the artist's conception of a totally imaginary horse, or it might represent an unregistered brand.

Nobody ever revealed the identity of those men who masked themselves and lynched Big Nose George on the streets of Rawlins. Only a couple of hints are available, but nothing was ever verified.

An Irishman named McCarien posted a note in the newspaper days later that stated, "Any person who says I put the rope around Big Nose George's neck Tuesday night is a willful and malicious liar."[24] McCarien had lived in Wyoming since it was part of Dakota Territory. Four months after the message, in mid-July, the same Charles McCarien was dead from mountain fever and nervous prostration. According to the paper, he may have had a rough manner, but in his breast beat a warm heart.[25] He had been ill even before the lynching, so his death at this time may just be a coincidence.

Then in December 1883, the same season B.T. Ryan, a good friend of the slain officers, offered the reward for the Widdowfield and Vincent's murderers who were still at large, the *Carbon County Journal* speculated on Ryan's possible role in Parott's lynching.[26] If Ryan was involved, he may have been the man in the white mask, but no proof was offered.

A.G. Edgerton, Carbon County Coroner, held his inquest on the body of Big Nose George Parott in Rawlins on March 23, 1881.[27] Sheriff Miller was still out of town. The coroner's jury included R.M. Galbraith, Frank Blake, Perry L. Smith, D.W. France, D.P. Hughes, and S.M. Miller. Several individuals had been subpoenaed to testify on the matter, including Samuel Simms, C.M. Scribner, J.E. Osborne, J.K. Orr (who was sick), A. Gear, Sam T. Lewis, William Daley, and J.C. Davis. These witnesses were a veritable Who's Who of successful men in Carbon County, but McCarien and Ryan were not questioned. All of the masked men remain unidentified to this day.

The Lynching of Big Nose George at Rawlins Wyo. in the Year of 1881 This Drawing is from a Description of the Lynching by a Witness.

Thomas Rooney's sketch of Big Nose George lynching in Rawlins shows a horse in the foreground branded Two Bar S. At the time it was thought it could be a clue as to the identity of one of the lynchers but no record was found of its registration. *Courtesy, Wyoming State Archives.*

Defense attorney S.T. Lewis opened the testimony at the inquest by stating that the crowd started going toward Hugus's store around 11:00 P.M., after he heard noise from the assault at the jail. Then he described the lynching before stating that Big Nose George had given his name as George Francis Warden.

According to Lewis's sworn coroner's testimony, Parott was born on April 8, 1843, near Dayton, Ohio.[28] Lewis further stated he did not think it was of any use to ask the crowd to cease and desist their vengeance on the criminal, so the lynching played out. He then identified the body as George Parott, the man whom he had defended against the recent murder indictment.

Sam Simms testified about having had a gun drawn on him while guarding the jail when the vigilantes broke in and grabbed Parott. Later, Simms was later standing about sixty feet west of the pole where Parott was hanging and mentioned the presence of about a dozen masked men. Scribner who also was in town on the night of the lynching, watched from about seventy-five feet away, and described the scene as presented here. A. Gear was a night switch operator for the railroad and had witnessed the lynching, but claimed it was too dark to see much. He did hear about three shots fired fifty feet from his position.

J.C. Davis apparently witnessed the lynching through a window while inside the Hugus and Company store. He later went to the Maxwell House after the execution. Deputy Daley then testified that John Signor came to his house and went up to the jail with him. Signor operated a small store out by the Sweetwater on the freight road between Rawlins and Lander at a place called Rongis, which was spelled by reversing the letters in John's last name. Daley and Signor found Jim and Joe Rankin at the jail and all the prisoners in their cells except Parott who had been taken away. He then left the Rankin boys in charge of the jail and later heard that someone was implicated in taking Parott's shackles.

Simms and inmate James Averell both told Daley that they could identify the man who had taken the shackles, which may imply the shackles had been taken off Parott at the jail before he was walked to the telegraph pole. Daley subsequently put the shackle thief, who never was named, in jail and turned the key over to the jailer.

Then Joe Rankin and Daley went to Hocker's, from there to Miller's, and afterward looked around the outside of the jail building, but nothing else was amiss there, other than the fact Parott had been removed. Daley could think of no more investigating needed, so he went to bed about midnight, but later was awakened by the coroner who requested Daley follow him to the telegraph pole and cut down the outlaw's body. They discovered the rope was about half an inch to five-eighths inch diameter and still stretched around Parott's neck. His neck had not been broken, indicating the outlaw died of strangulation.

The coroner's inquest deliberations ended with Daley's testimony, and the jury concluded with an inquisition oath. They recorded that: "George Parott, alias Big Nose George, was forcibly taken from the jail—taken from there to a telegraph pole—and thus hung by the neck with a rope—until he was dead—by a party of masked men to us unknown."

Dr. John Osborne took possession of Big Nose George's body shortly after the inquest was completed. Dr. Maghee did not return to Rawlins from an out-of-town trip until Thursday morning, March 24, two days after the lynching.

On April 9, 1881, the *Carbon County Journal* reported with levity when they looked over the original warrant for the execution of Big Nose George. The warrant, they mused, had been returned to proper authorities because it was not implemented. On the day of the appointed execution, George Parott could not be found in Carbon County.[29]

Katrine Hadsell, Sheriff Miller's youngest daughter, was born in 1894 and was my great-aunt. She remembered a story her father told her about the Big Nose George incident. Apparently, some local citizens came by Ike's home after he returned from Sand Creek a couple of days after the lynching and presented him with a sack they claimed had been placed around Big Nose George's head when he was hanged. Katrine remembered the item, but did not recall what happened to it.

Dr. John Osborne was a new young doctor in Rawlins working with Dr. Maghee on the body of Big Nose George. Osborne eventually became Wyoming Governor and a U.S. Congressman. *WikiCommons Photograph.*

Some citizens apparently still had not yet had their fill of the events of March 22, 1881. On Monday, April 4, a couple of men in town hung the stuffed effigy of a man on the same telegraph pole from which Big Nose George had been hanged several days earlier. Conductor J.C. Harrington was checking his train Number Five early Tuesday morning when he happened to glance up, then ran away, thinking it was another dead man. He never stopped to record any more train numbers on his way to the depot, where he reported seeing Big Nose George's ghost.[30] He must have thought Parott was an outlaw revenant.

An interesting development occurred in the summer of 1881. A letter sent to Governor Hoyt from the Consul General of France in

New York, asked for a copy of Parott's death certificate. The letter, received on August 11, had been initiated by the widow of George Parott, and the Consul General wanted a certificate of death for the convict to present to her. E.S.N. Morgan, Secretary of Wyoming Territory, forwarded the letter to J.W. Meldrum, Clerk of District Court in Laramie.[31]

Nothing seems to have come from this correspondence, which may not have been answered. Nonetheless, the possibility of a French connection with the outlaw has stimulated much interest. An article written in French claims the outlaw was a man born in that country.[32]

Earlier, on Friday, July 9, the county commissioners visited the home of Bob Rankin, still slowly recuperating from his head injuries. They presented his wife, Rosa, with a gold watch and chain for her bravery during Parott's attempted escape. Judge Homer Merrell made the presentation. Mrs. Rankin was overtaken with gratitude and offered her thanks to the group.

Engraved on the inside lid of the watch was: "Presented to Mrs. Rosa Rankin by the Board of County Commissioners of Carbon County, for bravery in preventing the escape of Big Nose George from jail March 22d, 1881."[33] James G. Rankin also expressed his thanks and appreciation. The timepiece eventually was given to Carbon County Museum, where it can be seen today. By 1918 Mrs. R. Rankin (probably Rosa) was living in Rawlins on Spruce Street,[34] the same year she passed away.

Chapter Six

The Restless Corpse

THE BIG NOSE GEORGE saga easily could have ended with his death at the hands of an angry vigilante mob, as did that of other outlaws who suffered vigilante justice. But it did not. Authorities placed his body in a simple coffin after the inquest, in case relatives came forward to claim it, but nobody did.[1] George's fate then became atypical. In fact, the most grotesque and remarkable aspects of his legacy were yet to be realized.

Dr. John Osborne had only lived in Rawlins a couple of weeks when he took possession of Parott's body. He moved the corpse to Dr. Thomas Maghee's medical office near the corner of Fourth and Cedar Streets, just a block north of Front Street. The two doctors decided in Maghee's office what to do next.

Osborne first made a plaster-of-paris cast of the outlaw's head, a so-called death mask. The ears are missing on the object; they may have scraped away while Parott hung by a rope from the telegraph pole or someone may have taken them as a post-mortem souvenir. The plaster likeness depicts the outlaw's broken nose, deflected to the left, as well as his mustache. Based on a cursory study of other western outlaw deaths from the late nineteenth century, this death-mask, found today at the Carbon County Museum, may be the only early West outlaw death mask available for contemporary research.

Lillian Heath, who later would become Wyoming's first female doctor, was a young assistant of Dr. Maghee's at the time. She was born in 1865, and her family moved to Wyoming in 1873, where her father worked for the Union Pacific.[2] Lillian's dad was interested in the medical field and assisted Dr. Maghee over the years with various treatments. Her father's enthusiasm piqued her own curiosity, and she became fascinated with medicine, so much so that Lillian herself began helping Maghee with patients in his Rawlins office. This included assisting with initial work on Parott's cranium.

Parott's cadaver exam began with a standard practice of the times. Maghee, with the assistance of Heath, and insistence of Osborne, sawed off Parott's skullcap to expose the brain for closer scrutiny so medical science could attempt to understand the criminal thought process. A similar practice was conducted only a year later by other medical professionals when they studied the brain of Charles J. Guiteau, assassin of President James A. Garfield in Washington, D.C.[3] Guiteau's brain was studied by medical experts,[4] then afterward it remained in the custody of medical professionals back east, along with his bones.[5]

The Rawlins physicians working on Parott probably followed the brain dissection recommendations published in *Gray's Anatomy*, which had been available to doctors since the first edition, titled *Anatomy*, was published in 1858. Gray states that:

"To examine the brain with its membranes, the skull-cap must be removed. In order to effect this, saw through the external table, the section commencing, in front about an inch above the margin of the orbit, and extending, behind, to a little above the level with the occipital protuberance. Then break the internal table with the chisel and hammer, to avoid injuring the investing membranes or brain; loosen, and forcibly detach the skull-cap, when the dura mater will be exposed. The adhesion between the bone and the dura mater is very intimate, and much more so in the young subject than in the adult."[6]

—·—

Once Big Nose George's skullcap was separated from the rest of his cranium, Dr. Osborne gave the cap to the teenage protégé, Lillian Heath, who kept it in her possession for nearly seventy years. The brain study itself apparently did not produce publishable results, because no details of the analysis have been discovered. Up to this

The doctors first made a death mask of Big Nose George's head. *Rick Weathermon photo, Courtesy, University of Wyoming Human Remains Repository.*

point, the two Rawlins physicians simply had undertaken a common dissection practice to learn what they could about criminal behavior from an investigation of a murderer's brain.

That part of Big Nose George's corpse contributed to science even if notes weren't taken, but the rest of his body did not fare nearly as well. Legends abound regarding the procedures Dr. Osborne used on his own to explore other parts of Parott's anatomy after he and Dr. Maghee finished the cranium study. Some of Osborne's actions produced artifacts now housed at museums so warrant attention because they contribute more direct evidence to the developing story.

Osborne skinned Parott's thighs and chest to acquire a sufficient amount of hide,[7] then had it tanned for further use. The young doctor made a pair of two-toned dress shoes using the man's skin for the lighter tone and cut leather for the darker tone. Persistent local and online accounts purport that he also made a medical bag and a coin purse from the tanned skin, however that cannot be verified and those items cannot be located.

An often-repeated story is that Osborne wore the shoes made from Big Nose George's tanned skin to his inaugural ball in Cheyenne when he took office as Wyoming's Governor shortly after statehood.[8]

Osborne made a "comic-opera" of taking office after his election, according to Wyoming historian T.A. Larson.[9] The Rawlins Democrat had faced a contentious election, followed by a delay in the official notice of results as the votes were counted. Impatient for the final outcome, Osborne directed a Cheyenne notary public to take his oath, then entered the Governor's Office where he issued a proclamation that he was "duly and legally qualified as governor."[10] Not until December 8, 1892, six days after Osborne took over the Governor's Office, did the canvassing board finally declare he had been elected, at which time he took a second oath of office.

While still a medical doctor in Rawlins long before his gubernatorial election, Osborne continued to work on Parott's corpse for about a year, keeping the dismembered body in a whiskey barrel filled with a salt solution. Osborne left the body in the barrel after he finished his "experiments," then buried it in a shallow unmarked grave in the yard behind Dr. Maghee's office in Rawlins, probably sometime in 1882.

The Big Nose George story slows down for awhile after Osborne's procedures, but never entirely left the collective memory of Rawlins. Citizens there and elsewhere still recalled the outlaw decades later, but few, if any, knew details regarding final disposition of the body.

Fifty-five years after the interment, former Governor John E. Osborne received a letter from Nina Moran, State Librarian. Dr. Osborne had moved back to Rawlins following his political career and read Moran's letter, which addressed a controversy that had arisen among historians in the state.

The State Historical Society received an unidentified human mandible (jaw bone) after they received Rosa Rankin's commemorative watch (the one later given to the Carbon County Museum). Rankin's daughter, Mrs. J.T. Williams of Oakland, California, had initially given the watch to the Wyoming State Library and Historical

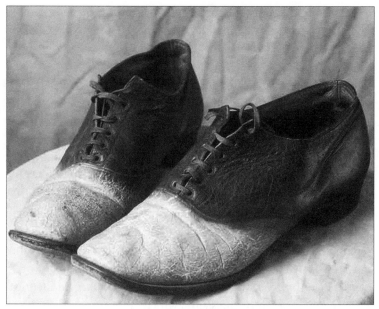

Dr. Osborne arranged for shoes to be made from Parott's tanned skin and cut leather from another source. *Courtesy, Carbon County Museum.*

Department. The mandible in question was given to the Historical Department by a George E. Abbott, of Cheyenne, who had received it from Robert W. Breckens some forty year earlier. Nothing else is known about Abbott or Breckens, and the mandible they relinquished was eventually discovered not to be that of the outlaw George Parott.[11]

However during the correspondence, Moran asked Dr. Osborne whether or not Lou Nelson (by then Dr. Lillian Heath's husband) also had a mandible purported to be Parott's. Moran knew the Heaths had a portion of the skull given to Lillian decades earlier by Osborne and wondered if she had a mandible as well. Moran asked Osborne to settle the matter.

Osborne replied with a short message typed along the margin of Moran's letter and sent it back to her. He stated, "I regret very much that it will not be possible for me to furnish the information for which a request is made in this letter."[12] The response is signed with

Osborne's flourishing signature. For some reason, he chose not to share his knowledge regarding the whereabouts of Big Nose George's skeletal remains.

—•—

The period between 1920 and the outbreak of World War II constituted tough economic times in Rawlins and elsewhere in the country. By then, second and third generation Rawlinsites went about their daily business with only occasional shared reminiscences regarding the Elk Mountain incident of 1878 and its aftermath. Robert Widdowfield had family in the area around Carbon, so his headstone monument and gravesite in that town's cemetery received regular care and attendance. Vincent apparently had been a single man with no relatives this side of Jefferson County, Iowa, where his parents and siblings lived before the family dispersed.[13] He probably had been a friendly loner of sorts when he lived in Rawlins.

Friends of both Widdowfield and Vincent had erected identical monuments for each of the slain lawmen. Vincent's was placed in the Rawlins cemetery but was not visited with nearly the frequency of Widdowfield's marker at Carbon. Sheriff Ike Miller's youngest son, Isaac Kirk Miller, my grandfather, took it upon himself to deliver flowers to Vincent's grave every May in the decades before World War II. He brought along his only daughter, Marguerite, and his youngest son, Frank, who was my father. Both of these children recalled in their later years the annual trips to Vincent's grave with their father when they were kids, him teaching each of them respect for the lawman and that Tip Vincent should not be forgotten.

The post-war Baby Boom hit Rawlins hard like it did most communities after World War II. Servicemen came home, got married, and started their families. Towns like Rawlins responded by improving transportation routes, offering town lots to veterans, expanding retail shops and service centers, and building new facilities to enhance the growing municipality. By 1950, the town was expanding beyond its early roots, and former city blocks were changing with new and better configurations.

Dr. Ben Sturgis, on the left, and Lou Nelson hold Parott's skullcap and cranium refit after the barrel discovery in 1950. *Courtesy, Carbon County Museum, Rawlins, Wyoming.*

On Thursday, May 11, 1950, workmen were excavating behind the new Hested's store on West Cedar in downtown Rawlins when Mike Gravouc, the backhoe operator, suddenly ceased digging.[14] Phil Wallstrom, general superintendent of the Metcalf Construction Company out of Omaha looked at the trench wall to see what caused the work stoppage. Embedded in the sediments of the trench profile was an old whiskey barrel rotting with age and laying horizontal a few feet beneath the ground's surface.

Curious citizens gathered in the alleyway between Fourth and Fifth Streets to watch the proceedings, having come from their own work places, restaurants, and other haunts when they heard of the unusual discovery. They stared into the excavation as Wallstrom opened the wooden lid to the barrel at 12:30 P.M., revealing its contents. The crowd gasped at a jumbled pile of disarticulated human bones staring back at them. A cranium whose skullcap had been sawn off lay with the other bones, but the skullcap was absent.[15] The barrel itself was not reported to have any identifying label either etched or glued onto its exterior.

Dr. Lillian Heath holds Big Nose George's skullcap in Rawlins circa 1950. She had kept the skullcap in her office. *Courtesy, Carbon County Museum, Rawlins, Wyoming.*

Ed Bennett, a Rawlins merchant among the onlookers that day, quickly made a connection between the skeleton and the nineteenth-century outlaw Big Nose George. Bennett knew that Dr. Lillian Heath of Rawlins possessed the skullcap of an outlaw, a man hanged nearly seventy years earlier. Lou Nelson (Heath's husband) brought the skull top to the discovery scene and, along with Dr. Ben Sturgis, Carbon County Coroner, held it next to the cut around the skull found in the whiskey barrel. The two bones fit together perfectly. They belonged to the same individual.

Lillian Heath recalled that back in the early 1880s Osborne had offered her a piece of Big Nose George's skin, but she had asked for a bone instead. This conversation proves that Osborne was not concealing his treatment of Parott's remains from at least some interested parties. Osborne gave Heath the skullcap instead of some skin, and it had been in her possession ever since, ensuring a strong, uninterrupted chain of custody. The true identity of the skeleton in the

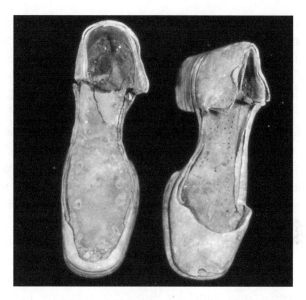

This pair of cut-up boots were found in the barrel with Parott's remains. It is possible that they provided part of the leather for the two-tone shoes Dr. Osborne had made. *Author photo.*

barrel was so obvious that Coroner Sturgis answered in the negative when asked if he would hold an inquest.

Workmen cleaned out the contents of the barrel, found some badly rotted cloth fabric, and what was then identified as a pair of shoes. On further inspection, the shoes proved to be the heels and soles from an old pair of cowboy boots whose upper shaft leather had been cut away and removed. They resembled the boots of a pauper; the rivet pattern on the soles did not even seem to match. Knowing they were buried with Big Nose George begs the question of whether or not Dr. Osborne had earlier cut the boot leather from them to use in the manufacture of his famous two-tone shoes.

The newspaper added that the barrel also mysteriously contained an empty bottle of Lydia F. Pinkham's Vegetable Compound. Pinkham's solution in the late nineteenth century was a well-known women's tonic for treatment of menstrual and menopausal problems, now largely debunked as a legitimate remedy by many medical experts.[16] Someone may have tossed the bottle into the barrel before it was closed over Big Nose George as a final insult to his manhood.

Lieutenant Harry Forney, of the Rawlins Police Force, took possession of the barrel contents then placed them at the police department for safekeeping. Coroner Sturgis suggested that all of the barrel contents be given to the Carbon County Museum, but museum officials that night were undecided about whether or not to accept the gift.[17] The remains already emitted an unpleasant odor, and discussion may have centered on ethical considerations in the treatment of a human skeleton. However, no mention of reburial in an established cemetery was recorded. By now, Parott apparently was recognized more as a legend and less as a human being.

Eventually the county museum accepted some of the barrel contents and kept the lower skull in their facility in the Carbon County Courthouse for a time. Sheriff John Terrill apparently took possession of the post-cranial bones for disposition sometime in the early 1960s. For the second time the resting place of the bones of Big Nose George seems uncertain. Local accounts suggest they may have been buried in an unmarked grave at the outskirts of town or dropped from an airplane over either the Red Desert or Utah. Dr. Osborne apparently gave Big Nose George's death mask and the shoes to the Rawlins National Bank where they were on display for several years. He gave the outlaw's shackles to the Union Pacific Museum in Omaha in 1928.[18]

Both the death mask and Osborne's infamous shoes eventually found their way to the Carbon County Museum in Rawlins in 1982, along with the jail register that recorded Big Nose George's confinement. Dr. Lillian Heath asked that the skullcap be given to the Union Pacific Museum to be held with the shackles. The infamous outlaw would never be in just one place ever again.

Chapter Seven

A Cranial Encore

M cMAHAN, in her graduate work, points out that the media sometimes reports inaccurate information in their haste to get a story in print, and this is never more true than with the legend of George Parott.[1] Even the discovery of the barrel caused quite a stir in the press. The media began exploiting the fantastic episode of Parott's life the day after the barrel was opened when a local merchant advertised a product sale in the *Rawlins Daily Times* newspaper under the headline: "'Big Nose' lost his scalp with these low prices."[2] Mention of the outlaw quickly became a marketing tool.

More recently, other public outlets have incorporated aspects of the outlaw legend into their own media coverage. In one case, authors included mention of a pair of granger style boots that had been donated to the Wyoming State Museum with a note stating they belonged to Parott.[3] Further research by the museum staff showed they were stamped inside with "J. McCowan" and were accessioned as part of a military collection from the general period of the Spanish American War, unrelated to the outlaw.[4] Researchers know from direct physical evidence that an entirely different pair of damaged boots had been buried in the barrel along with the outlaw's skeleton, and it is reasonable to conclude he was wearing that pair when he was hanged.

Another example of popularized legend comes from a sporting goods firm that sells replica firearms made in Italy. In one of their catalogs a couple of decades ago, they promoted a model 1860 Lawman, forty-four caliber revolver, listing that it was like the weapon carried by the outlaw Big Nose George.[5] But researchers have not yet identified the actual weapons used by the outlaw, and no primary evidence that he owned this particular handgun style has come to light.

———

Perhaps the most obvious evolution of the Big Nose George story into pure literary fiction is Allan Vaughan Elston's 1958 novel *Wyoming Manhunt*.[6] Elston opens chapter two with Parott's confession at Carbon, where the outlaw names himself and only three accomplices to the Widdowfield/Vincent murders. They were Dutch Charley Burris, Jack Campbell, and the totally fictitious Homer Hatch. The rest of the book unfolds with the dangerous manhunt for Hatch throughout the territory.

These and other fanciful or unsubstantiated aspects of the outlaw's life have permeated business marketing, media coverage, and historical summaries over the past 140 years. The popularity of such cultural mythology harkens back to the accuracy embedded in the epigraph from "Liberty Valance" mentioned at the beginning of this book. When given a choice between legend and fact, many people will prefer to believe the more colorful legend.

But, what of the irrefutable characteristics of the real outlaw? These deserve more attention as well. Three specific pieces of physical evidence establish the true identity of George Parott as the outlaw variously known as Big Nose George, George Reynolds, and George Francis Warden.

First is his cranium, taken directly from Parott's articulated skeleton by Dr. Osborne, sawn in two, and the skullcap given to Lillian Heath before Osborne buried the rest of the skeleton in the backyard. Heath's sole possession of the skullcap established a solid chain of custody used to confirm that the human remains found in 1950 belonged to the outlaw hanged in 1881. Additionally, the skullcap is much better preserved than the rest of the skull to which it fits, illustrating stark differences in bone preservation between the two types of contexts in which each portion reposed between 1881 and 1950.

Second is the death mask. Osborne admitted he made a death mask of the outlaw that remained in his possession until he turned it over to the Rawlins National Bank, who eventually gave it to the Carbon County Museum. The death mask had been formed directly from the head of Parott's corpse before any surgery, and it preserves distinctive facial characteristics of the outlaw hanged on March 22, 1881, in Rawlins.

The third piece of evidence is the portrait photo of Big Nose George as he looked the year before his death. Presumably this image was used to confirm the outlaw's identity at the time of his arrest and trial, and many Rawlins residents were familiar with the photo. It probably was taken in Omaha in 1880 and circulated in the community to illustrate what Parott looked like during his final months in Rawlins.

The limited physical evidence of these three objects prompted an attempt in 1995 to further investigate the Parott story. Scientists at the Department of Anthropology, University of Wyoming, and the Office of the Wyoming State Archaeologist collaborated in the examination. The first order of business was securing loans of the artifacts from the Union Pacific Museum in Omaha and the Carbon County Museum in Rawlins to gather the available items for study in the campus lab.

The research team consisted of four colleagues. Dr. George Gill, now a Professor Emeritus, conducted the biological and forensic investigation. Dr. Rick Weathermon, a Professional Research Scientist, performed specific bioarchaeological comparisons. Kristi McMahan (now Kristi McMahan Nunn), a graduate student at the time, wrote a class paper in Public Archaeology and a Physical Anthropology Area Paper summarizing several of our findings. As Wyoming State Archaeologist in 1995, I directed three field investigations for the project, one at the trestle site near Robbers' Roost, one at the ghost town of Carbon, and the third at the murder scene in Rattlesnake Canyon.

Our collaborative effort resulted in the first time in forty-five years that Parott's two skull parts had been in one place. We initially

In 1950 a portion of the remains of George Parott were discovered buried in a barrel in a Rawlins alley. *Courtesy, Carbon County Museum, Rawlins, Wyoming.*

wanted to confirm that the two skull parts refit, which they did. Then we wanted to compare the refit cranium to both the death mask and the portrait photo to look for shared visual attributes of shape and dimension.

Weathermon prepared photographic superpositions of the loaned artifacts. The skull and death mask could be rotated as three-dimensional objects for comparative photographs, but the flat portrait photograph was fixed in its two-dimensional perspective. This meant Weathermon had to move the skull, then the death mask, into angles similar to that shown on the portrait image, to get comparable photos for each superposition.

All three superpositions—(1) skull–death mask, (2) skull–portrait photo, and (3) death mask–portrait photo—strongly suggest they represent the same person, the outlaw George Parott. The rest of our 1995 study documented discrete and metric traits from Parott's refit cranium to help expand our knowledge of his physical identity.

We already had some help from the *Carbon County Journal* from August 14, 1880, where a reporter described the physical appearance of the recently jailed outlaw for the readership.[7] He claimed the outlaw gave his real name as George Francis Warden. He further stated the accused was about thirty-five years old, stood five-feet, ten-inches tall, was sparsely built, and weighed about 160 pounds. The outlaw had a beard, sharp piercing eyes, and a prominent roman nose. The hair color, eyes, and nose described by the reporter are supported by evidence in the portrait photo as well as a black and white photograph possibly can.

The beard presumably referred to Parott's mustache unless he had grown a beard after the portrait photo was taken in Omaha. Most of the outlaws in the Powder River Gang wore considerable facial hair.

Parott's post-cranial bones were disposed of in the 1960s, so our 1995 investigations could not measure any long bones for stature to confirm the reporter's height estimate. Nor could we study any unique injuries, wounds, or anomalies on them.

Author Engebretson[8] illustrates a spent bullet held at the Wyoming State Museum, said to have been taken from Big Nose George's body. Such a gunshot wound may have caused visible bone damage, but this possibility can no longer be addressed, which is unfortunate because osteological analysis of skeletal trauma in early white frontier populations has long been a productive avenue of research.[9]

The estimated age of thirty-five years offers some testable applications in our physical analysis of his cranium, the only remaining bones from his skeleton. Testimony at Parott's coroner's inquest also helps, where Attorney Sam T. Lewis said Parott had told him he was born on April 8, 1843 near Dayton, Ohio.[10] This birthdate puts Parott a couple of weeks short of his thirty-eighth birthday when he was hanged on March 22, 1881.

The 1995 bioarchaeology and forensic lab work resulted in productive findings. Left to right: Dr. George Gill, Kristi McMahan Nunn, Dr. Mark Miller. *University of Wyoming photo, Courtesy, Human Remains Repository.*

A separate French source says the Wyoming outlaw actually was George Frederik Parrot, born in France on March 20, 1834, who left behind a wife and child when he emigrated to the United States.[11] Apparently, his birth certificate suggests this individual would have been two days short of forty-seven years old when the outlaw George Parott died in Wyoming, but the connection between these two individuals is not yet proven.

The marital status of Parott in this French publication is consistent with the information provided in the 1881 letter from the French Consul to the Governor of Wyoming, relaying a wife's request for a copy of Parott's death certificate. Dr. Gill even indicated that the large nose on Parott's skull suggests he may be of French Mediterranean descent.[12] This possible connection deserves further research.

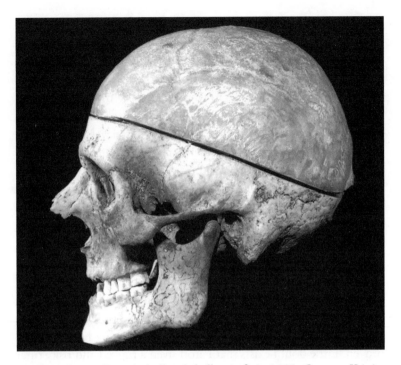

Big Nose George Parott's skull and skullcap refit in 1995. *Courtesy, Kristi McMahan Nunn.*

Dr. Gill's 1995 forensic analysis builds on these historical sources. He assigned data base number DB139 to the Parott sample on loan to the university, and then looked at tooth eruption and wear on the maxillary (skull) and mandibular (jaw bone) teeth to derive an age estimate. Gill also assessed the pattern of cranial suture closure for the same purpose. Taken together, these skeletal data suggest an age range of thirty-five to fifty at time of death, which is consistent with both the age supplied at the coroner's inquest and in the French publication. Bone porosity of the cranium also indicated middle age.

Gill's interorbital feature measurements—taken around the eye sockets and nasal bones—plus visual observations, identified the cranial morphology as that of an adult, white (Caucasoid) male.[13] A prominent chin and sharp nasal sill helped establish this conclusion.

Gill also noted a previous fracture in Parott's prominent nose, where it deflected to the left, probably sometime before death.

In addition to recording osteometric data on Parott,[14] Gill discussed an interesting dental anomaly first recognized by former Rawlins dentist Dr. William E. Scoggin who x-rayed the mandibular teeth. Scoggin ascertained that the second deciduous molars are present bilaterally as the second permanent premolars never formed. The permanent first premolars are present on each side and fully erupted. The maxillary and mandibular third molars were not present and probably never formed. In addition, Parott was missing his mandibular four incisors and the jawbone was fully healed, so they may have been lost before death in an accident such as a horse kick or fist fight.[15] This and other scientific evidence are available elsewhere.[16]

Parott's excessive occlusal wear and tooth staining suggest a few behavioral factors. His rural diet probably included foods that gathered abrasive material when they were transported and prepared, thus wearing down his teeth prematurely when he ate. The staining suggests a habit of chewing tobacco, though this has not been proven. Little doubt exists that Parott lived a rugged and risky rural lifestyle the last few years of his mortal existence.

Osborne's two-toned shoes also were available for our 1995 study. The Wyoming State Crime Lab inspected them visually and concluded that the lighter toned material was consistent with the texture of human flesh. We took this avenue of research no further because to do so would have required destructive analysis.

The fact that Parott's skull has survived all this time may open additional doors for future research, such as DNA study if enough interest is shared by the relevant institutions who control the specimens. Permission already was given to Dr. Gill in 1995 by the Union Pacific Museum to sample hair and tissue removed from the skullcap in their possession. This sample, as well as bone and teeth from the cranium, hold potential to yield enough DNA for a genetic profile, perhaps either with mitochondrial or Y-chromosome samples. A lab in Oklahoma has expressed a willingness to consider performing this test if permissions are obtained. However, all parties who claim Parott's remaining physical evidence must agree to some level of destructive analysis, with no real assurance that a test will produce positive results.

A separate, comparative sample might be drawn from possible modern descendants, if they exist, to help establish the outlaw's true pedigree. A few families already have researched missing nineteenth-century ancestors from the Wyoming area and have inquired about Parott in their search. None of these individuals, however, have established a biological connection with the outlaw or produced a DNA sample. Each one completed their ancestry research with other genealogical sources. DNA may help resolve theories like the suggestion that Parott immigrated to the U.S. from France and left a family behind. Perhaps his dental anomalies also may yield clues to ancestry.

Even so, DNA research could be a dead end, and interested parties may not even agree to attempt it. Factors such as cost, accuracy, and privacy must be considered. Future scholars may want to expand this investigation further if the opportunity arises.

Matching grave headstones for Tip Vincent and Robert Widdowfield still exist. Vincent's, on the left, can be found in the Rawlins Cemetery and Widdowfield's in the Carbon Cemetery. *Author photos.*

Afterword

◦

Trail's End at Last?

OVER 140 YEARS have elapsed since Big Nose George Parott burst onto the scene in Carbon County, Wyoming. Murder, mayhem, and macabre experiments have driven public interest in his story ever since. Sensational qualities inherent in the episode evoke strong sentiments in each generation they reach and color the cultural history of nineteenth-century Rawlins.

By the new millennium, those early-day residents had passed away. Today's local citizens are lifetimes removed from the troublesome affair. But, even with the passage of time, the legend of George Parott continues to haunt our collective memory. Details of his career survive in public venues and draw curiosity seekers visiting the town to enjoy the rich heritage. Big Nose George has grown more popular as a legend than he ever was as a man.

A great irony dwells in part of the tragic outlaw story of the Powder River Gang. Rawlins residents reviled George Parott, but citizens of Gallatin, Missouri, sympathized with his criminal partner Frank James and never investigated his potential role in the Wyoming murders.

In fact, James's own trial for an unrelated murder convened in 1883 in Missouri, where he benefited from a much stronger and more aggressive defense team than Parott had received in Wyoming three years earlier. Their overall litigating strategy earned James's acquittal. Then, sometime after being exonerated, Frank James traveled the lecture circuit in comfort with Cole Younger, detailing the hazards of a life of crime to diverse audiences willing to listen. James never even faced the murder charge in Wyoming for which Carbon County had indicted him and for which Parott had been hanged.

———

Readers of western history may never know to an absolute certainty where Frank James was between July 1878 and April 1879. Since he was the best-known outlaw named in the Widdowfield/Vincent murders, his true whereabouts during the crime has the potential to stimulate real controversy. The debate regarding the question of Frank's Wyoming presence is well established in literature.

Several writers have taken a stand on the subject, but first-hand eyewitness accounts are rare indeed, and what conclusions are drawn in secondary treatments typically lack clear, unambiguous source attribution, making them difficult to verify. This dilemma is true for many of the pro and con references written decades after the Elk Mountain incident.

However, at least two authors writing in the late 1870s and early 1880s, argue that Frank and his brother Jesse spent some of the time between 1876–1879 in Texas.[1] Breihan, in his 1974 seminal work on the James brothers, concurs with the Texas destination, and adds that the two men also traveled to Mexico, even though he discusses Frank's acquaintance with Big Nose George in 1878.[2] Gladys Beery, writing in 1993, concludes the James boys were not in Wyoming Territory.[3]

In contrast, sources supporting Frank James in Wyoming during this period are equally compelling. Atwell quotes from O.P. Hanna's diary; Hanna was a man who arrived in the Big Horn area in 1878 who said, "Jesse James and his gang had a hideout in the Little Goose Creek Valley, not far from the new Fort McKinney…."[4] Atwell goes on to speculate that the proximity to the fort may explain James's choice of his alias, McKinney.

May Davis-Howard wrote a letter to her nephew in the 1930s telling him the story of her arrival to the Big Horn area in the summer of 1879 when she was ten years old. It involved a message she and her father took to O.P. Hanna. There they met a Black man named John who cooked for "rounders" she identified as the "Jesse James Outlaws." She recalled:

""Mr. Foster gave Pa a letter of introduction to Oliver Hanna who lived on Goose Creek. When we reached there, Little Goose Creek was running bank full. But we crossed just above the bridge at Skinners. We drove by a two-room log cabin and a big log barn. ...John came out delighted to see us. He was the cook for a bunch of rounders. In a year or so, the rounders and John disappeared. (...John had belonged to a uncle named Wilfey. The rounders were part of the Jesse James Outlaws)."[5]

In 1982, Patterson argued not only that Frank James was in on the murders of Widdowfield and Vincent, but that he also spent the winter of 1878-1879 in southwestern Wyoming.[6] His brother Jesse joined him there.

While the few contemporary sources mentioned above are important, the most convincing evidence comes from primary District Court documents in Carbon County. Frank James was indicted for the Elk Mountain murders following a legally constituted Grand Jury hearing in that county. J.W. Meldrum, Clerk of District Court, filed three indictments between April 1879 and December 1880 naming Frank James as one of the accomplices, Criminal Case numbers 265, 266, and 271.[7] James also had been named as a gang member by George Parott in his parlor statement, which was ruled by the court as his true admission to the crime for which he was charged.

The most important variable in this debate is not whether researchers in the twenty-first century can prove Frank James was in Wyoming back then. What matters is the fact that Big Nose George identified him as a gang member, and Carbon County law enforcement indicted him as an accomplice in the crime spree of August 1878. The most important element, then, is that contemporary sources believed he had been here.

Carbon County could have solved the question of his whereabouts simply by extraditing James from Missouri to stand trial in Rawlins where the legal system could have established his innocence or guilt. Since James was not extradited, we will let the readers decide for themselves whether or not he was involved.

—·—

Why was the legal outcome of George Parott's case so radically different from that of Frank James in Missouri.? Both men had been tried for murder. Both men had been indicted for shooting a weapon into the chest of Tip Vincent, killing him instantly. But both were not treated the same while in custody. Parott was jailed, tried, and condemned to death for his crime. His mental condition became so rattled after the blistering prosecution case, he argued for his own guilt and punishment, nullifying any opportunity for his defense team to present a favorable case.

Following Parott's attempted jail break, some Carbon County residents became singularly responsible for his brutal ligature strangulation on Front Street in Rawlins. The vigilante lynching had been a slow, drawn-out death, and more painful than his scheduled legal execution would have been, but the end result was the same— George Parott was dead.

Rawlins vigilantes performed this same type of execution on Opium Bob and Lacey only a year later, which taken together with the George Parott incident, helped prompt the larger community to organize a police force that would assist the sheriff in law enforcement. This decision was a major step in the social maturity of the community.

Parott's own story didn't end with his death. His macabre, postmortem treatment sets him apart in the annals of outlaw history in the American West. Why did Osborne perform such diabolical dismemberments, when by all accounts he otherwise was a successful, leading citizen? He eventually was elected Governor of Wyoming as a Democrat and then as a Congressman in the United States House of Representatives.[8] As Governor, he seemed to have been a strong advocate of the rule of law, particularly as it pertained to ensuring safe passage during the transfer of criminal suspects between states.[9] The man must have had some empathy for the less fortunate.

Osborne only had been in Rawlins for a couple of weeks prior to Parott's demise. The outlaw sat in jail for months before the doctor even arrived in the Territory, so neither man had sufficient time to become personally acquainted with the other. No records show that the doctor ever visited the prisoner in his cell. They must have been nearly strangers at the time of Parott's death.

Once Parott's body was removed to Maghee's medical lab after the coroner's inquest, Osborne performed his experiments on the corpse. Then, even before Frank James was lecturing to the masses about the evils of crime, George Parott's skin had been fashioned into shoes worn by Governor John Osborne at his inaugural ball. The way of the transgressor proved to be unpredictable indeed.

Parott enjoyed no romantic "lost cause" around which to rally public sympathy like that surrounding Frank James. Parott was not known in Wyoming for anything greater than the crimes for which he was convicted. He was neither as smart as Frank James nor as lucky. Even so, it baffles credibility that James never was extradited to Wyoming to stand trial for Vincent's murder, even when relevant local authorities knew his whereabouts during the Missouri trial. After all, the man already was in custody there and was the subject of widespread public reporting.

Carbon County authorities probably worried about paying expenses for extradition or more reward money, though a couple of local residents had offered to cover the latter for Powder River Gang members still at large. Authorities also may have anticipated difficulties and expense in a lengthy prosecution if they faced the proven effectiveness of James's defense team. Or maybe they thought that this man in Wyoming was a different Frank James than the one in Missouri.

Perhaps the Big Nose George lynching left a sour taste in the mouths of Carbon County residents, and they simply hoped to move on from the entire affair. Whatever the reason, if given the go-ahead, Sheriff Miller could have traveled to Missouri to serve legal papers on James and returned to Rawlins with the suspect in custody to stand trial. Since James never testified, his alleged role in the Widdowfield/Vincent murders was never clarified in court. Frank James's role, if any, in the George Parott crime spree remains one of the most challenging aspects of this story.[10]

This book postulates that Frank did indeed take part in the 1878 Wyoming crime spree, which is a plausible scenario. What is certain is that his presence in Wyoming is not the product of fanciful myths developed by twentieth-century authors and western historians. The suspicion of his involvement came from individuals living in Wyoming in the 1870s, who identified Frank James in contemporary statements.

May Davis-Howard had visited the Little Goose Creek cabin with her father and met the Black cook in 1879. The April 1879 murder indictments list Frank James as an accomplice; one claims he shot Tip Vincent in the chest. Parott named James as a gang member. The accumulation of such circumstantial evidence prompted me to offer the explanatory model of the crime spree that I have. If primary evidence ever emerges that proves a different explanation, I will happily adjust my theory.

How then does a community's sense of justice reflect in its social character after nearly a century and a half have passed? Should myths take precedence over historical facts? Will truth about the whole Parott affair ever overshadow his colorful legend? These questions permeate the social character of Rawlins today as it comes to grip with how to portray the Elk Mountain affair as a crucial episode in its local history.

Pure evil saturates the incident, but the naked reality is that wickedness pervades both Parott's malicious criminal behavior as well as Osborne's extreme post-mortem experiments. A complete, unvarnished history must come to grips with this fact, and people must deal honestly with both behaviors.

Historian Mike Cassidy[11] argued that to understand the true character of an outlaw, an investigator must ask who were his victims and what laws were violated. In the case of Big Nose George, the answers are simple. Robert Widdowfield and Henry Vincent were two popular men employed by legitimate public interests to investigate a probable crime against society. While the unsuccessful derailment of a train may not rise to a major offense, the two homicides clearly violated the legal norms of the time.

Parott did not escape conviction for his behavior in Rattlesnake Canyon as Frank James did for alleged similar behavior in Missouri shortly thereafter. The social context for James in Missouri seemed drastically different from that for Parott in Rawlins. Such disparity in treatment between the two criminals makes one wonder if the greatest basis for punishment of a crime is not so much what a person did, but where he did it.

Rawlins changed in the seventy years between Parott's death and the discovery of the bone-filled barrel in the alley. An entirely different generation was in charge of community decisions in 1950 than in 1881, even if a few old-timers like Lillian Heath remained. Very few living residents in 1950 would have had first-hand knowledge of the Parott crime spree or witnessed his punishment. They may not even have known about Osborne's disposal of the body after the outlaw's death, since Osborne was silent on the subject in later years.

One assumes this later generation would have had a more re-strained opinion of Parott at the time of the barrel discovery than the earlier generation had when the man was lynched. But, instead of interment of the body in the penitentiary cemetery like other convicted criminals received, part of his skull was given to the county museum for public exhibit, part to the Union Pacific Museum, and the rest of the skeleton was discarded. The power of the Big Nose George legend continued to influence community decisions even in the mid-twentieth century.

Today, with an even newer generation of citizens, we can ask broader questions about that history. Should we consider giving Parott's few surviving mortal remains a proper burial, assuming all relevant scientific evidence has been obtained from them? The Carbon County Coroner originally gave part of the outlaw's skull to the museum. Perhaps that same office could work with the museum to deaccession those remains and inter them in the cemetery at the old Wyoming State Penitentiary, with the permission of the State of Wyoming, who is the property owner. Parott's name could be inscribed on a marker where public visitation is allowed. The notoriety of the outlaw's criminal past might even enhance public interest in further preserving the penitentiary grounds.

Rawlins has taken valuable steps in recent decades to rectify formerly insensitive matters. The county museum removed Parott's cranium from public exhibition and replaced it with a full-sized plastic cast of the refit skull. His actual lower skull and jaw are in secured storage, and the museum staff indicates they will not be placed on exhibit again. This status simplifies a transfer to cemetery interment if the community so desires.

American principles themselves have changed in the last few decades. Increased cultural sensitivity is particularly evident in the treatment of human skeletal remains inadvertently discovered outside established cemeteries. Museums across the country have relinquished collections of American Indian remains for repatriation and reburial and given back other objects as well.[12] This trend alone warrants a closer look at the George Parott situation.

Another problematic question can be addressed. Are people open to the remote possibility that Parott may have living descendants? Is it even a viable avenue of research, given the nature of privacy issues and the history of Parott's post-mortem story? Public support for DNA research may help resolve identity questions one way or the other. But, would establishing Parott's ancestry help define his identity and close the book on any mystery, or would it exacerbate it? These are questions to ponder in the long term.

Regardless of what more we learn about Parott's early life, what happened to him at and after death reflect as much on our social character as on the convict himself. We are rightly embarrassed by the vigilante lynching and some of Osborne's post-mortem techniques. Neither event really did anything to fulfill the legal judgment rendered against Parott in court. His legally executed hanging and subsequent burial would have done so much more to end the Big Nose George story and prevent the growth of his troublesome legend.

In 1996, an event in the historic promotion of Carbon County encapsulated the community's emotional struggle to incorporate George Parott's story into a Rawlins revitalization project. City authorities agreed to build a public park across Front Street from the refurbished Union Pacific Railroad Depot, so they called for proposals.

The controversy began when they received an architect's drawing of a statue proposed for the park. Who was depicted in the drawing, but Big Nose George Parott.[13] The resulting discussion of the project drew concern from several sections of the community. Many people were opposed to erecting a statue of the outlaw.

One Rawlins resident, L.E. (Steve) Stevens, a great nephew of the murdered Robert Widdowfield, expressed deep concern about the plan. He argued that any monument should commemorate the two murdered lawmen, Robert Widdowfield and Tip Vincent, instead of the convicted outlaw who helped murder them. Objections by Stevens and others settled the controversy for a time, and the statue was not built.

More recently, community members erected a large billboard prominently depicting the notorious outlaw on horseback and including much smaller illustrations of objects and events related to his story. At this writing, it stands adjacent to the Railroad Depot in the vicinity of Parott's lynching site and across the street from the new Depot Park. The two law enforcement officers are represented on it by a small drawing in one corner of the billboard, dwarfed by the prominent image of a mounted Big Nose George.

As a former Rawlins resident, whose great-grandfather was sheriff when Parott died, I like the idea of a Widdowfield/Vincent statue in Depot Park. Although photographs of the two lawmen have not been found that would help establish their individual physical features, it would be easy enough to erect a statue using what personal details are available.

Their lack of suitable recognition on our cultural landscape is the greatest failure in the Big Nose George legend, and the most important fact of the case yet to receive adequate public attention. A Widdowfield/Vincent statue would bring some balance to the whole story of the Elk Mountain affair and supplement the current emphasis on the outlaw visible around town, including the tasteful interpretive exhibit of Parott in the Carbon County Museum.

Other than a small monument erected at the murder scene in Rattlesnake Canyon on private land, there is no suitable memorial for the two lawmen who died while in service to the citizens of Wyoming Territory. They deserve explicit acknowledgment in the county's historic architecture, someplace where the bulk of its citizens can view artistic likenesses of them. Even Parott himself expressed remorse for their deaths and admitted that justice for them should be served. What better way than a statue dedicated to their service while tracking the outlaw gang from Powder River?

These few ideas would go far to blur the specter of Big Nose George's legend and place his memory deeper into the factual context of history. Until then, the fanciful aspects of his life and death will continue to taint an accurate and comprehensive heritage of law enforcement in Wyoming. Otherwise, Parott's legend has no place to rest nor will its power over this place ever be mitigated. The unselfish bravery of these two outnumbered lawmen deserves to be the center of the Big Nose George story rather than relegated to its periphery. Ford's movie was partly correct ... this *is* the West folks. But, when a legend becomes fact, print the fact.

Endnotes

Preface

1. Daniel Y. Meschter, *The Rankins of Rawlins: A Family Biography.*
2. Max R. Atwell, *Ambush on Elk Mountain: The Murders, the Manhunt, and Big Nose George Parott.*
3. Lewis R. Binford, *Working at Archaeology*, pp. 45-53.
4. Kristina E. McMahan, "Violence on the Frontier: Case Study, Big Nose George."

Cast of Characters

1. David Throgmorton, *Savagery and Civilization: George Parrot, Governor John Osborne and Curious Justice on the Frontier*, pp. 68-71.

Chapter 1. A Sinister Cloud Gathers

1. Bennett H. Stein, *Tough Trip Through Paradise: Montana 1878*, p. xiii.
2. Stein, p. 7.
3. Engebretson, *Empty Saddles, Forgotten Names*, p. 112.
4. Stein, p. 33.
5. For Northfield, see Mark Lee Gardner. *Shot All to Hell: Jesse James, the Northfield Raid, and the Wild West's Greatest Escape.* For Wyoming, see Richard Patterson, *Wyoming's Outlaw Days*, p. 18.
6. James P. Muehlberger, *The Lost Cause: The Trials of Frank and Jesse James*, p. 101.
7. Gary A. Wilson, *Outlaw Tales of Montana*, p. 115.
8. I.S. Bartlett (editor), *History of Wyoming, Vol. 1*, p. 604. Agnes Wright Spring, *The Cheyenne and Black Hills Stage and Express Routes*, p. 253. May Davis-Howard, 1930s letter to Fred Hilman of Big Horn. Christina Schmidt, "Famous James brother made camp in Big Horn," *The Sheridan Press.*
9. Carl W. Breihan, *The Escapades of Frank and Jesse James*, p. 28-43, 218.
10. Davis-Howard, 1930s letter to Fred Hilman.

11. Dorothy M. Johnson, *The Bloody Bozeman: The Perilous Trail to Montana's Gold*, pp. 4-5, 14-21, 326-327.

12. Mark E. Miller, *Military Sites in Wyoming 1700-1920: Historic Context*, pp. 87-98.

13. Robert M Utley, *Frontier Regulars: The United States Army and the Indian, 1866-1891*, pp. 121-122.

14. G.L. Holt, *Holt's New Map of Wyoming*. Adapted from the General Land Office.

15. Mermardi, Deputy Surveyor, General Land Office field notes subdivisions 1888-1897, Col 196, 1882.

16. Meschter, *Carbon County Chronology*, *Sentinel* 10(26), May 30, 1878.

17. Meschter, *Carbon County Chronology*. *Sentinel* 10, Mon. June 3, 1878. The posse consisted of Deputy Sheriff James G. Rankin, Deputy Sheriff Robert Widdowfield, William Daley, Jesse Wallace, E. Webber, William McCarty, Jens Hanson, William Aylsworth, Thomas B. Jones, L. Calvert, and J. B. Adams. The Percy bandits were John Thomas, D.H. Hill, William Henry, and W.H. Gibson.

18. Meschter, *Carbon County Chronology*. *Sentinel* 10(26), May 30, 1878.

19. Margaret Brock Hanson (editor), *Powder River Country: The Papers of J. Elmer Brock*, p. 159.

20. Coroner's Inquest on the Body of Charles Bates (AKA Dutch Charley), January 7, 1879. Frank Howard testimony.

21. Spring, pp. 190-191.

22. Spring, pp. 252-253. Additional bandits included Jackson Bishop and, possibly, Persimmon Bill.

Chapter 2. A Failed Robbery and Two Cold-Blooded Murders

1. John H. Ostrom and John S. McIntosh, *Marsh's Dinosaurs: The Collections from Como Bluff*, p v.

2. Mark Jaffe, *The Gilded Dinosaur: The Fossil War Between E.D. Cope and O.C. Marsh and the Rise of American Science*, p. 234.

3. John H. Ostrom and John S. McIntosh, page 16.

4. Meschter, *The Rankins of Rawlins*, p. 35.

5. Meschter, *Carbon County Chronology*, *Daily Sun* 4 (171), Thursday, July 15, 1875.

6. Meschter, *The Rankins of Rawlins*, p. 35.

7. Meschter, *The Rankins of Rawlins*, p. 33.

8. Michael F. Kohl, and John S. McIntosh, *Discovering Dinosaurs in the Old West: The Field Journals of Arthur Lakes*, pp. 88-91. Ostrom, John H. and John S. McIntosh, p. 28.

9. Patterson, *Historic Atlas of the Outlaw West,* p. 57.

10. Mary Lou Pence, *Boswell: The Story of a Frontier Lawman,* p. 114.

11. *Testimony in the Case of the Territory of Wyoming v. George Parott.* Taken on November 17, 1880.

12. *Testimony Wyoming v. Parott,* November 17, 1880.

13. Coroner's Inquest, Henry H. Vincent. J. B. Adams testimony, August 29, 1878.

14. Meschter, *The Rankins of Rawlins,* pp. 18-24.

15. L.E. "Steve" Stevens, personal communication, Rawlins, WY, 1996,

16. Coroner's Inquest, Henry H. Vincent. I.M. Lawry testimony, August 29, 1878.

17. Meschter, *The Rankins of Rawlins*, pp. 33-36.

18. Meschter, *The Rankins of Rawlins.*

19. *Laramie Daily Sentinel,* V. 10, No. 204, December 27, 1878.

20. Throgmorton, p. 159.

21. Coroner's Inquest, Robert Widdowfield, August 29, 1878, in Carbon, Wyoming.

22. Paul Sierson, local historian. Saratoga, WY: personal communication, Summer 1982.

23. Throgmorton, p. 139.

24. L.M. Lampton, *GLO record.* The surveyor on the day of the murders.

25. Officer Down Memorial Page, www.odmp.org.

26. *Laramie Daily Sentinel,* August 24, 1878.

27. *Laramie Daily Sentinel,* August 27, 1878.

28. *Laramie Daily Sentinel,* August 27, 1878.

29. *Laramie Daily Sentinel,* August 28, 1878.

30. *Carbon County Brand Records,* RG 1047, Vol. A 1872-1881, and Vol. B 1872-1893.

Chapter 3. Outlaw Diaspora

1. Spring, pp. 261-263.

2. Pence, p. 117.

3. *Laramie Daily Sentinel,* December 23, 1878.

4. Frye, pp. 62-74.

5. Pence, pp. 124-125.

6. Meschter, *The Rankins of Rawlins,* p. 37.

7. Frye, pp. 64-65.

8. Meschter, *The Rankins of Rawlins,* p. 38.

9. Coroner's Inquest, Charles Bates, January 7, 1879. Frank Howard testimony.

10. Pence, pp. 129.

11. *Laramie Daily Sentinel,* January 10, 1879.

12. Coroner's Inquest, Charles Bates, John S. Jones testimony.

13. Coroner's Inquest, Charles Bates, Jens Hanson testimony.

14. Coroner's Inquest, Charles Bates.

15. Coroner's Inquest, Charles Bates, Hanson testimony.

16. Carbon County Court criminal complaint against John Minuse (alias Joe Minuse) for murder. Territory of Wyoming v. Joe Minuse #264.

17. Carbon County Court murder indictment for Joe Minuse et al., April 7, 1879. Criminal Case #265.

18. Murder Indictment, John Minuse, April 7, 1879.

19. Affidavit accompanying Criminal Case No. 265 in Territory v. John Minuse.

20. Verdict against John Minuse, September 10, 1879.

21. Frye, pp. 73-74.

22. Carbon County Court Indictment for the Murder of Robert Widdowfield, April 7, 1879. Criminal Case No. 266.

23. Carbon County Court Indictment for the Murder of Henry H. Vinson (Vincent), April 7, 1879. Criminal Case No. 271.

24. Affidavit by Charles D. Torrey regarding the murders of Widdowfield and Vincent, September 11, 1879.

25 . Patterson, *Wyoming's Outlaw Days,* p. 22.

26. Muehlberger, pp. 153-184.

27. Frye, p. 65.

28. *Carbon County Journal,* May 23, 1885 and August 1, 1885.

29. Engebretson, p. 116.

30. Mark E. Miller, "Big Nose George Parott: On the Cold Trail of an Outlaw."

31. Engebretson, pp. 117-118.

32. Engebretson, pp. 117-118

33. Engebretson, pp. 118-119.

34. Meschter, *The Rankins of Rawlins,* p. 63.

35. Throgmorton, p. 143.

36. Maurice Kildare, "Big Nose George's Loot," *Lost Treasure* (magazine), p. 11.

37. Meschter, *The Rankins of Rawlins*, p. 63.

38. Atwell, p. 98.

39. Daniel Y. Meschter, *The Rankins of Rawlins,* p. 63-65. M. Wilson Rankin, *Reminiscences of Frontier Days.* Atwell, pp. 97-114.

40. Doug Engebretson, p. 111.

41. Frye, p. 81.

42. *Carbon County Journal*, August 14, 1880.

43. *Carbon County Journal*, August 14, 1880.

44. Carbon County Jail Register.

Chapter 4. The Territory of Wyoming v. George Parott

1. *Carbon County Journal*, September 4, 1880.

2. Virginia Cole Trenholm (editor), *Wyoming Blue Book*, Vol. 1, p. 337.

3. *100 Years in the Wild West: A Pictorial History of Rawlins, Wyoming.*

4. *Laramie Daily Sentinel*, March 3, 1875. Daniel L. Kinnaman, *Rawlins, Wyoming: The Territorial Years, 1868-1890*, p. 96.

5. Ann Gorzalka, *Wyoming's Territorial Sheriffs*, p. 159.

6. Daniel L. Kinnaman, p. 96.

7. Meschter, *The Rankins of Rawlins*, p. 25.

8. *Historic Downtown Walking Tour: Walking Through History.*

9. Meschter, *The Rankins of Rawlins*, p. 71.

10. *100 Years in the Wild West: A Pictorial History of Rawlins, Wyoming* and *Reflections: A Pictorial History of Carbon County*, pp. 166-169.

11. Trenholm, *Wyoming Blue Book*, pp. 285-286.

12. Meschter, *The Rankins of Rawlins*, p. 73.

13. *Carbon County Journal*, September 18, 1880.

14. *Carbon County Journal*, September 25, 1880.

15. Meschter, *The Rankins of Rawlins*, p. 74.

16. *Carbon County Journal*, September 25, 1880.

17. *Carbon County Journal*, October 16, 1880.

18. *Carbon County Journal*, November 20, 1880.

19. Affidavit in Support of Motion for Change of Venue, November 8, 1880.

20. Meschter, *The Rankins of Rawlins*, p. 74.

21. *Carbon County Journal*, November 13, 1880.

22. *Carbon County Journal*, November 20, 1880.

23. Quarterly Bulletin (*Annals of Wyoming*), "Chapman Diary." Vol. 1, Nos. 1&2: pp. 7-9.

24. Muehlberger, p. 163.

25. *Carbon County Journal*, November 20, 1880.

26. Criminal Case No. 265, supporting documents.

27. L.E. "Steve" Stevens, Stevens Family Tree.

28. Maxwell House Register, 1880.

29. Criminal Case No. 265, James Rankin testimony.

30. Criminal Case No. 265, William Daley testimony, page 20 in the original hand-written version.

31. Coroner's Inquest, Robert Widdowfield, August 29, 1878, Carbon, WY.

32. Criminal Case No. 265, M. F. Leech testimony.

33. *Carbon County Journal,* November 20, 1880.

34. Meschter, *The Rankins of Rawlins,* p. 75.

35. *Carbon County Journal,* November 20, 1880.

36. John W. Blake, Willis Van Devanter, and Isaac Caldwell (editors), *Revised Statutes of Wyoming Territory*, p. 275.

37. Criminal Case No. 265. Indictment for the Murder of Henry H. Vincent.

38. Blake, Van Devanter, and Caldwell (editors), *Revised Statutes of Wyoming Territory*, p. 274.

39. *Carbon County Journal,* December 18, 1880.

40. *Carbon County Journal,* December 18, 1880.

41. Criminal Case No. 265, supporting documents.

42. *Carbon County Journal,* December 18, 1880.

43. Criminal Case No. 265, indictment and supporting documents.

44. *Carbon County Journal,* December 18 1880.

45. Abstract of Docket Journal Entries, The Territory of Wyoming v. George Parott.

46. *Carbon County Journal,* January 15, 1881.

47. *Carbon County Journal,* December 18, 1880.

Chapter 5. Ligature Asphyxia

1. *Carbon County Journal,* January 8, 1881.

2. *Carbon County Journal,* February 12, 1881.

3. *Carbon County Journal,* January 15 and 22, 1881.

4. Spring, pp. 288-289.

5. *Carbon County Journal,* January 29, 1881.

6. *Carbon County Journal,* February 19, 1881.

7. *100 Years in the Wild West.*

8. *Carbon County Journal,* March 5, 1881.

9. *Carbon County Journal,* March 12, 1881.

10. *Carbon County Journal,* March 12, 1881.

11. *Carbon County Journal,* March 19, 1881.

12. *Carbon County Journal,* March 26, 1881.

13. Daniel Y. Meschter, *Sweetwater Sunset: A history of the lynching of James Averell and Ella Watson near Independence Rock Wyoming on July 20, 1889.*
14. *Carbon County Journal,* March 26, 1881.
15. *Carbon County Journal,* March 26, 1881.
16. *Carbon County Journal,* March 26, 1881.
17. *Carbon County Journal,* March 26, 1881.
18. *Carbon County Journal,* March 26, 1881.
19. *Carbon County Journal,* March 26, 1881.
20. *Carbon County Journal,* March 26, 1881.
21. *Carbon County Journal,* March 26, 1881.
22. Doug Engebretson, p. 124.
23. Red Garrison, former State Brand Inspector. Laramie: personal communication, Summer 2004.
24. *Carbon County Journal,* March 26, 1881.
25. *Carbon County Journal,* July 16, 1881.
26. *Carbon County Journal,* December 15, 1883.
27. Coroner's Inquest, Big Nose George Parott, March 23, 1881.
28. Coroner's Inquest, Big Nose George Parott, March 23, 1881.
29. *Carbon County Journal,* April 9, 1881.
30. *Carbon County Journal,* April 9, 1881.
31. Letter from A. Lefaiore, Consul General of France, August 11, 1881. Letter to Hon. J.W. Meldrum from E.S.N Morgan, August 20, 1881. *Cheyenne Daily Leader,* August 20, 1881.
32. Boris Massaini, *Aux USA, le bandit montbeliardais transforme en Chaussures!*
33. *Carbon County Journal,* July 9, 1881. Carbon County Museum, *The Legend of Big Nose George,* p. 7.
34. 1918 *Rawlins City Directory,* p. 49.

Chapter 6. The Restless Corpse

1. Throgmorton, p. 185.
2. Kathryn McKee, "Unwritten Chapters: Professional Contributions of Women During Settlement of the Rocky Mountain West," *Annals of Wyoming,* 91(3), 2019, pp. 16-17.
3. *Carbon County Journal,* July 1, 1882.
4. *Carbon County Journal,* July 8, 1882.
5. Wikipedia.org/wiki/Assassination_of_James_A._Garfield.
6. Henry Gray, *Gray's Anatomy,* p. 617.

7. *The Legend of Big Nose George,* p. 6-7.
8. *The Legend of Big Nose George,* p. 7.
9. T.A. Larson, *History of Wyoming,* pp. 287-288.
10. Larson, p. 287.
11. Letter from Nina Moran, State Librarian, to John E. Osborne, November 1, 1937.
12. Moran Letter, November 1, 1937.
13. Meschter, *The Rankins of Rawlins,* p. 35.
14. Atwell, p. vi.
15. *Rawlins Daily Times,* May 12, 1950.
16. Wikipedia, https://en.wikipedia.org/wiki/Lydia_Pinkham#Lydia_E._Pinkham's_Vegetable_CompoundLydia.
17. *Rawlins Daily Times,* May 12, 1950.
18. *Rawlins Daily Times,* May 12, 1950.

Chapter 7. A Cranial Encore

1. Kristina E. McMahan, "Anthropology and the Media Case Study: Big Nose George Parrott," p. 5.
2. *Rawlins Daily Times,* May 13, 1950, p. 3.
3. Tom Lindmier, and Steve Mount, *I See by Your Outfit: Historic Cowboy Gear of the Northern Plains,* p. 43.
4. Jim Allison, Wyoming State Museum, Supervisor of Collections, personal communications, 2021.
5. *Cabela's Master Catalog,* Spring 1997, p. 368. For comparison, the Sweetwater County Museum in Green River, Wyoming, exhibits a Remington cap and ball, .44 caliber revolver, New Model 1858 Army, given to them in 1969 by the son of a man who was county sheriff there from 1933–1942, Accession Number 69-81-19. It purportedly belonged to Big Nose George Parott.
6. Allan Vaughn Elston, *Wyoming Manhunt.*
7. *Carbon County Journal,* August 14, 1880.
8. Engebretson, p. 124.
9. George W. Gill, "Skeletal Injuries of Pioneers." In *Skeletal Biology in the Great Plains: Migration, Warfare, Health, and Subsistence,* pp. 159-172.
10. Coroner's Inquest, George Parott, March 23, 1881.
11. Boris Massaini, Aux USA, *le bandit montbeliardais transforme en Chaussures!*
12. Lori Van Pelt, *Dreamers & Schemers: Profiles from Carbon County, Wyoming's Past.*
13. George W. Gill, "Caucasoid Racial Differentiation-Interorbital Features Method."

14. George W. Gill, "Three-Page Osteometric Data Sheet."

15. McMahan, "Violence on the Frontier: Case Study Big Nose George Parrott," p. 18. Dr. William Scoggin, written correspondence, August 6, 2021.

16. Rick L. Weathermon (editor), *Tales from the Trails: Bioarchaeology and 19th Century Wyoming.*

Afterword: Trail's End at Last?

1. Hon. J. A. Dacus, Ph.D., *Life and Adventures of Frank and Jesse James, the Noted Western Outlaws*, pp. 326-327. Anonymous, *Jesse James: The Life and Daring Adventures of this Bold Highwayman and Bank Robber,* pp. 63-65.

2. Breihan, *The Escapades of Frank and Jesse James*, pp. 28-43, 205-216.

3. Gladys Beery, *Sinners and Saints: Tales of Old Laramie City*, pp. 185-191.

4. Atwell, pp. 189-190.

5. May Davis-Howard, The Davis Family manuscript.

6. Patterson, *Wyoming's Outlaw Days,* pp. 18-23

7. Criminal Case Number 265. Indictment dated April 7, 1879, for the murder of Henry H. Vinson. Criminal Case Number 266. Indictment dated April 7, 1879, for the murder of Robert Widdowfield. Criminal Case Number 271. Indictment dated April 7, 1879, for the murder of Henry H. Vinson.

8. Trenholm (editor), pp. 472-473.

9. *Public Papers, Messages, and Proclamations, Hon. John E. Osborne, Governor of Wyoming,* 1893-1894, pp. 72-76.

10. Robert K. DeArment, *Assault on the Deadwood Stage: Road Agents and Shotgun Messengers*, pp. 237-238.

11. Mike Cassidy, "The American Outlaw in Social Context: A Brief Introduction."

12. Federal Historic Preservation Laws, Native American Graves Protection and Repatriation Act, pp. 166-182.

13. *Laramie Daily Boomerang,* June 1, 1996, p. 7.

Bibliography

100 Years in the Wild West: A Pictorial History of Rawlins, Wyoming. Rawlins, WY: Rawlins Daily Times, 1968.

Anonymous. *Jesse James: The Life and Daring Adventures of this Bold Highwayman and Bank Robber, and His No Less Celebrated Brother, Frank James, Together with the Thrilling Exploits of the Younger Brothers.* Philadelphia: Barclay & Co., 1882.

Atwell, Max R. *Ambush on Elk Mountain: The Murders, the Manhunt, and Big Nose George Parott.* Tucson, AZ: Max R. Atwell, 2013.

Bartlett, I.S. (editor). *History of Wyoming, Vol. I.* Chicago: The S.J. Clarke Publishing Company, 1918.

Beery, Glayds B. *Sinners and Saints: Tales of Old Laramie City,* pp. 185-193. Glendo, WY: High Plains Press, 1994.

Binford, Lewis R. *Working at Archaeology,* pp. 45-53. New York: Studies in Archaeology, Academic Press, 1983.

Blake, John W., Willis Van Devanter, and Isaac Caldwell (editors). *Revised Statutes of Wyoming Territory.* Cheyenne: The Daily Sun Steam Printing House, 1887.

Breihan, Carl W. *The Escapades of Frank and Jesse James.* New York: Frederick Fell Publishers, Inc., 1974.

Cabela's Master Catalog. Sidney, NE: Cabela's Inc., Spring 1997.

Carbon County Brand Records, RG 1047, Vol. A 1872-1881, and Vol. B 1872-1893, AS Location 899. Cheyenne: Wyoming State Archives.

Carbon County Jail Register. Rawlins: Carbon County Museum.

Carbon County Journal. Newspapers, 1879-1881. Rawlins: Carbon County Museum.

Cassidy, Mike. "The American Outlaw in Social Context: A Brief Introduction." Typed manuscript, 1987. On file with author.

Cheyenne Daily Leader. Newspaper. Cheyenne: Wyoming State Archives, microfilm.

Coroner's Inquest on the Body of Henry H. Vincent, August 29, 1878. Rawlins: Carbon County Clerk of District Court.

Coroner's Inquest on the body of Robert Widdowfield, August 29, 1878. Rawlins: Carbon County Clerk of District Court.

Coroner's Inquest on the Body of Charles Bates (AKA Dutch Charley), January 7, 1879. Rawlins: Carbon County Clerk of District Court.

Coroner's Inquest on the Body of Big Nose George Parott, March 23, 1881. Rawlins: Carbon County Clerk of District Court.

Criminal Case No. 265. Carbon County Court murder indictment for Joe Minuse et al., April 7, 1879. Rawlins: Carbon County Clerk of District Court.

Criminal Case No. 265, indictment, testimony, change of venue affidavit, and supporting document. Rawlins: Carbon County Clerk of District Court.

Criminal Case No. 266. Carbon County Court Indictment for the Murder of Robert Widdowfield, April 7, 1879. Rawlins: Carbon County Clerk of District Court.

Criminal Case No. 271. Carbon County Court Indictments for the Murder of Henry H. Vinson (Vincent), April 7, 1879. Rawlins: Carbon County Clerk of District Court.

Dacus, Hon. J.A., Ph.D. *Life and Adventures of Frank and Jesse James the Noted Wetern Outlaws.* St. Louis: W.S. Bryan, Publisher, 1880.

Davis-Howard, May. "The Davis Family: A letter to Fred Hilman of Big Horn written by May Davis-Howard, 1930s." Typescript copy from Ross Hilman on file with the author.

DeArment, Robert K. *Assault on the Deadwood Stage: Road Agents and Shotgun Messengers.* Norman: University of Oklahoma Press, 2011.

Elston, Allan Vaughn. *Wyoming Manhunt. Pocket Books, Inc.,* New York: Lippincott Edition, 1958.

Engebretson, Doug. *Empty Saddles, Forgotten Names.* Aberdeen, SD: North Plains Press, 1982.

Federal Historic Preservation Laws. *Native American Graves Protection and Repatriation Act,* pp. 166-182. National Center for Cultural Resources. Washington, DC: National Park Service, U.S. Department of the Interior, 2002.

Frye, Elnora L., *Atlas of Wyoming Outlaws at the Territorial Penitentiary.* Cheyenne: Pioneer Printing & Stationery, 1990.

Gardner, Mark Lee. *Shot All to Hell: Jesse James, the Northfield Raid, and the Wild West's Greatest Escape.* New York: Harper Collins Publishers, 2013.

Gill, George W. "Skeletal Injuries of Pioneers," in *Skeletal Biology in the Great Plains: Migration, Warfare, Health, and Subsistence,* pp. 159-172. Washington, DC: Smithsonian Institution Press, 1974.

_____ "Caucasoid Racial Differentiation-Interorbital Features Method." University of Wyoming, Worksheet, 1995. Copy on file with author.

_____ "Three-Page Osteometric Data Sheet, University of Wyoming." Worksheet. 1995. Copy on file with author.

Gorzalka, Ann. *Wyoming's Territorial Sheriffs.* Glendo, WY: High Plains Press, 1998.

Gray, Henry. *Gray's Anatomy.* Fifteenth Edition. New York: Fall River Press, 2013.

Hanson, Margaret Brock (editor). *Powder River Country: The Papers of J. Elmer Brock.* Cheyenne: Frontier Printing, 1981.

Historic Downtown Walking Tour: Walking Through History. A pamphlet. Rawlins: Rawlins Landmark Commission, 1994.

Holt, G.L. *Holt's New Map of Wyoming.* Adapted from the General Land Office. Cheyenne:, G.L. Holt, 1883.

Jaffe, Mark. *The Gilded Dinosaur: The Fossil War Between E.D. Cope and O.C. Marsh and the Rise of Science.* New York: Three Rivers Press, 2000.

Johnson, Dorothy M. *The Bloody Bozeman: The Perilous Trail to Montana's Gold.* New York: McGraw-Hill, 1971.

Kildare, Maurice. "Big Nose George's Loot" in *Lost Treasure,* February 1976, p. 11. Grove, OK: Lost Treasure, Inc., 1976. On file with author.

Kinnaman, Daniel L. *Rawlins, Wyoming: The Territorial Years, 1868-1890.* Rawlins: Kinnaman Supply, 2013.

Kohl, Michael F., and John S. McIntosh. *Discovering Dinosaurs in the Old West: The Field Journals of Arthur Lakes.* Washington, DC: Smithsonian Institution Press, 1997.

Lampton, L.M. "General Land Office Record, August and September, T19N, R82W." Surveyor on the day of the murders, 1878.

Laramie Daily Boomerang. Newspaper. Cheyenne: Wyoming State Archives, microfilm.

Laramie Daily Sentinel. Newspaper. Cheyenne: Wyoming State Archives, microfilm.

Larson, T.A. *History of Wyoming.* Lincoln: University of Nebraska Press, 1965.

The Legend of Big Nose George. Special Limited Edition. Rawlins: Staff and Board of the Carbon County Museum, 2004.

Lefaiore, A. "Letter from Consul General of France, August 11, 1881." Cheyenne: Wyoming Department of State Parks & Cultural Resources, State Archives.

Lindmier, Tom, and Steve Mount. *I See by Your Outfit: Historic Cowboy Gear of the Northern Plains.* Glendo, WY: High Plains Press, 1996.

Massaini, Boris. Aux USA, *le bandit montbeliardais transforme en Chaussures!* https://www.estrepublicain.fr/edition-belfort-heriCourt-montbeliard/2019/08/05/aux-usa-le-bandit-montbeliardais-transforme-en-chaussures. Accessed on January 9, 2021.

Maxwell House Register, 1880. Rawlins: Carbon County Museum.

McKee, Kathryn. "Unwritten Chapters: Professional Contributions of Women During Settlement of the Rocky Mountain West" in *Annals of Wyoming* 91(3):16-17. Cheyenne: Wyoming State Historical Society, 2019.

McMahan, Kristina E. "Anthropology and the Media Case Study: Big Nose George Parrott," p. 5. Paper in Public Archaeology (ANTH 5550). Laramie: University of Wyoming, 1996.

_____ "Violence on the Frontier: Case Study, Big Nose George." Physical Anthropology Area Paper. Laramie: Department of Anthropology, University of Wyoming, 1996. On file with author.

Mermardi, Deputy Surveyor. General Land Office field notes subdivisions 1888-1897, Col 196 1882. Online: accessed September 1, 2019.

Meschter, Daniel Y. *Carbon County Chronology. Sentinel* 10(26), May 30, 1878. Unpublished manuscript, 1970. On file in Rawlins: Carbon County Library.

_____ *Sweetwater Sunset: A history of the lynching of James Averell and Ella Watson near Independence Rock Wyoming on July 20, 1889.* Wenatchee, WA: Daniel Y. Meschter, 1996.

_____ *The Rankins of Rawlins: A Family Biography.* Albuquerque, NM: Daniel Y. Meschter, 2001.

Miller, Mark E. "Big Nose George Parott: On the Cold Trail of an Outlaw." Paper presented at the 62nd Annual Plains Anthropological Conference, Billings, MT: 13-16 October, 2004. On file with author.

_____ *Military Sites in Wyoming 1700-1920: Historic Context.* Laramie and Cheyenne: Wyoming Department of State Parks & Cultural Resources, 2012.

Moran, Nina. "Letter from Nina Moran, State Librarian, to John E. Osborne, November 1, 1937." Copy on file with author

Morgan, E.S.N. "Letter to Hon. J. W. Meldrum, August 20, 1881." Cheyenne: Wyoming Department of State Parks & Cultural Resources, State Archives.

Muehlberger, James P. *The Lost Cause: The Trials of Frank and Jesse James.* Yardley, PA: Westholme Publishing, 2013.

Officer Down Memorial Page, www.odmp.org. Accessed August 31, 2019.

Osborne, John E. *Public Papers, Messages, and Proclamations, Hon. John E. Osborne, Governor of Wyoming, 1893-1894.* C.P. Hill, private secretary, compiler. Cheyenne: Wyoming State Archives, 1894.

Ostrom, John H., and John S. McIntosh. *Marsh's Dinosaurs: The Collections from Como Bluff.* New Haven, CT: Yale University Press, 1966.

Parott, George. *Affidavit in Support of Motion for Change of Venue, November 8, 1880.* Clerk of District Court, Carbon County, Wyoming.

Patterson, Richard. *Historical Atlas of the Outlaw West.* Boulder, CO: Johnson Books, 1982.

_____ *Wyoming's Outlaw Days.* Wyoming Frontier Series. Boulder, CO: Johnson Books, 1985.

Pence, Mary Lou. *Boswell: The Story of a Frontier Lawman.* Cheyenne: Pioneer Printing & Stationery Co., 1978.

Quarterly Bulletin (*Annals of Wyoming*). "Chapman Diary." Vol. 1, Nos. 1 & 2: pp. 7-9. Cheyenne: State of Wyoming Historical Department, 1924.

Rankin, M. Wilson. *Reminiscences of Frontier Days.* Denver: Smith-Books, 1978.

Rawlins City Directory. Rawlins: Rawlins City Directory, 1918.

Rawlins Daily Times. Newspaper. Cheyenne: Wyoming State Archives, microfilm.

Reflections: A Pictorial History of Carbon County, pp. 166-169. Rawlins: Carbon County Museum, 1990.

Schmidt, Christina. "Famous James brother made camp in Big Horn." Sheridan: *The Sheridan Press,* June 13, 2014.

Scoggin, Dr. William. Email correspondence to the author, August 6, 2021. On file with author.

Spring, Agnes Wright. *The Cheyenne and Black Hills Stage and Express Routes.* Lincoln, NE: University of Nebraska Press, 1948.

Stein, Bennett H. *Tough Trip Through Paradise: Montana 1878.* San Francisco: Houghton Mifflin Company, Comstock Editions, Inc., 1948.

Stevens, L.E. "Steve." "Stevens Family Tree." Undated. On file with author.

"Territory of Wyoming v. George Parott (1880)" in *Abstract of Docket Journal Entries.* Rawlins: Carbon County Clerk of District Court.

Territory of Wyoming v. Joe Minuse (1879). Criminal Case No. 264. Criminal complaint against John Minuse (alias Joe Minuse) for murder. Rawlins: Carbon County Clerk of District Court.

Territory of Wyoming v. John Minuse (1879). Affidavit accompanying Criminal Case No. 265. Rawlins: Carbon County Clerk of District Court.

Territory of Wyoming v. George Parott, Testimony taken on November 17, 1880. Rawlins: Carbon County Clerk of District Court.

Throgmorton, David. "Savagery and Civilization: George Parrot, Governor John Osborne and Curious Justice on the Frontier." Unpublished manuscript, 2013. On file with the author.

Torrey, Charles D. Affidavit regarding the murders of Widdowfield and Vincent, September 11, 1879, Case 265. Rawlins: Carbon County Clerk of District Court.

Trenholm, Virginia Cole (Editor). *Wyoming Blue Book,* Vol. I. Cheyenne, Wyoming: Wyoming State Archives and Historical Department, 1974.

_____ *Wyoming Blue Book*, Vol. II. Cheyenne: Wyoming State Archives and Historical Department, 1974.

Utley, Robert M. *Frontier Regulars: The United States Army and the Indian, 1866-1891.* Lincoln: University of Nebraska Press, 1973. First Bison Book printing, 1984.

Van Pelt, Lori. *Dreamers & Schemers: Profiles from Carbon County, Wyoming's Past.* Glendo, WY: High Plains Press, 1999.

Weathermon, Rick L. (editor). *Tales from the Trails: Bioarchaeology and 19th Century Wyoming.* Manuscript in preparation for publication, 2021. On file with the editor.

Verdict of John Minuse, September 10, 1879. Rawlins: Carbon County Clerk of District Court.

Wikipedia.org/wiki/Assassination_of_James_A._Garfield. Wikipedia: Accessed on October 5, 2019.

Wikipedia.org/wiki/Lydia_Pinkham#Lydia_E._Pinkham's_Vegetable_CompoundLydia. Wikipedia: Accessed October 7, 2019.

Wilson, Gary A. *Outlaw Tales of Montana.* Havre, MT: High-Line Books, Montana, 1995.

Index

Davis, Charles 62
Davis, J.C. 101, 103
Deadwood, SD 31
Dickinson, Ed 37, 41, 43, 56, 79
Dutch Charley *see Bates, Charles*

— E —

Edgerton, A.G. 101
Elk Mountain, WY 19, 33-34, 40-
    41, 43, 51-53, 55-60, 63-65,
    67-70, 74, 78, 80, 82, 84-85,
    91, 112, 128, 129, 132, 135

— F —

Fieldhouse, Isaac 43
Foote, John 79-81
Foote's Ranch, WY 43, 45
Fort Fetterman, WY 29, 56, 67
Fort McKinney, WY first location
    30, 53
Fort McKinney, WY second loca-
    tion 26, 29, 31, 67, 128
Fort Steele, WY 30, 78, 82
Front Street in Rawlins 72, 98,
    100, 107, 130, 134

— G —

Garcia, Andrew 21-23
Gear, A 101, 103
Gill, George 119, 122-124
Green River, WY 22, 37, 58, 62,
    70, 91

— H —

Hadsell, Katrine 104
Hanson, Jens 60, 62
Harrington, Henry 57, 58,
Harrington, J.C. 105
Heath, Lillian 20, 107-108, 111,
    114, 116, 118, 133

Howard, Frank 31, 56-59
Hoyt, John 68, 105

— I —

Irvine, Tom 17, 66-67
Irvine, William H. 91

— J —

James, Frank "McKinney" 18, 23,
    25-26, 28, 30, 32, 39-40, 53,
    56-58, 62-65, 69-70, 78, 84-
    85, 127-133
James, Jesse 18, 23, 25-26, 40, 58,
    64, 128-129

— K —

Kearns, Ed 59

— L —

Lakes, Arthur 20, 38
Lampton, L.M. 50
Landon, John 97
Laramie, WY 18, 30, 41, 50, 55,
    57-59, 65, 69, 74, 106
Lawry, Ike 19, 29, 41, 43
Leech, M.F. 19, 70, 76, 78-80, 82-
    85, 88
Lefever, John 58
Lewis, Samuel T. 74-77, 80, 82-89,
    100-101, 103, 121
Little Goose Creek, WY 25-26,
    28-30, 32, 128-129, 132

— M —

Maghee, Thomas 20, 76, 79, 83,
    92, 104-105, 107-110, 131
Marsh, Othniel 20, 36
Masonic Building, Rawlins, WY,
    74, 78, 93
May, Boone 54, 91-92

Acknowledgments

⁘⸱•⸱⁘

This is a work of historical nonfiction. I have done my best to provide an accurate interpretation of the record of Big Nose George and have made careful inferences when needed to fill a chronological or behavioral gap in the sequence of events. My explanatory model hopefully serves as a fair telling of his past. This book could not have been completed without the support of several individuals, though any errors or omissions are mine alone.

First of all, I want to recognize three historians who piqued my early interest in the history of Carbon County and the outlaw George Parott. Dan Meschter, Rans Baker, and Dan Kinnaman paved the way for my research with their willing ideas and their own studies.

Lindy Musgrave Glode, former Clerk of District Court in Carbon County, made the original court transcripts, coroner's inquests, and supporting documents available to me many years ago. That data opened a fascinating door into the events of 1876–1881.

Carbon County Museum staff provided valuable input and showed me the artifacts they retain from the Elk Mountain affair and its aftermath. Ashlee James, Registrar, and Carol Reed were most gracious, helping me acquire the necessary photos to supplement my research. Carol also read an earlier version of this manuscript and offered valuable suggestions.

Years ago, Marybelle Lambertsen kick-started my earliest interest in Carbon County history by providing me full access to the bound set of the *Carbon County Journal* newspapers at the museum. They are a treasure trove of information on Parott and Rawlins.

Steve Sutter and Samuel Levin were quite helpful providing data from the Wyoming State Historic Preservation Office, Cultural Records. Sam worked diligently to help me prepare the State of Wyoming map.

I took three field trips with some colleagues to relevant archaeological sites pertaining to Big Nose George: the Como trestle, Carbon ghost town, and the murder scene in Rattlesnake Canyon. Brent Breithaupt, Rick Weathermon, and Beth Southwell helped with field investigations. Kristi McMahan Nunn also helped with an early survey of the railroad route between Medicine Bow and Como Bluff. Thanks to them and all the cooperating private land owners.

In addition to Kristi and Rick, my colleague in the Department of Anthropology, University of Wyoming, Dr. George W. Gill, performed the lion's share of biological and forensic work on Parott's skull when it was loaned to us in 1995. He is an expert in the study of early pioneer bioarchaeology, and I truly benefitted from hours of conversation with him. Thanks also to Dr. William Scoggin for his insights on Parott's dental array.

The Wyoming State Archives also provided valuable images and records to enhance preparation of the story. Carl Hallberg and Suzi Taylor were particularly useful, and I thank them. I thank every institution and individual that gave me permission to use images.

Jim Allison of the Wyoming State Museum provided grateful assistance in research on a pair of boots at their facility and in the background of one image. Thanks, Jim.

Several friends and colleagues have read early versions of my manuscript, and offered constructive suggestions for its improvement. My brother, Rod Miller, has a brilliant command of the English language and I appreciate his editorial comment. Dr. David Throgmorton, Dr. Barbara Robinson, and Dr. Rick Weathermon read and commented on the flow of the story. Rawlins Historian, Dan Kinnaman, also reviewed the work, as did Marcus Huff, a strong western history advocate. They all helped improve my prose.

Thanks to Lori Van Pelt for writing the foreword and to Dr. Phil Roberts, Paul Hedren, W. Michael Gear, and Kathleen O'Neal Gear for reading and commenting on my work. The strong support and work ethic of High Plains Press, under the capable leadership of Nancy Curtis and Laura McCormick, helped me through the tribulations of trying to publish historical nonfiction. Thank you both!

Author

⋯●⋯

M ARK E. MILLER was born in Rawlins and raised on his family's ranch. Mark's great-grandfather Isaac (I.C.) Miller was Carbon County Sheriff in 1880 when Big Nose George sat in jail awaiting his scheduled execution for the murder of lawman Henry H. "Tip" Vincent. This family connection inspired Mark to research the crimes of the notorious outlaw.

Miller received his B.A. and M.A. in Anthropology at the University of Wyoming and his Ph.D. in Anthropology from the University of Colorado in Boulder. He is an Adjunct Professor in Anthropology at the University of Wyoming and the retired Wyoming State Archaeologist, having served in that position from 1984–2014. Throughout his career he was a member of the Sigma Xi Scientific Research Society and the Phi Kappa Phi Honor Society. Miller was a Resident Fellow in the Ucross writing program in 2003.

Mark's other research interests include the prehistory of Wyoming and the early history of Carbon County, on which he has published extensively. He enjoys living along the banks of the Big Laramie River with his partner, Barbara, and the spectacular migratory birds that fly back and forth over the lush, green meadows, and quaking aspen.

NOTES ON THE PRODUCTION OF THE BOOK

This book was simultaneously released in two editions.

A *limited edition hardcover* of only 200 copies
with headbands of maroon and gold,
bound in Maroon Rainbow,
embossed with Winter Silver foil,
and wrapped in a full-color dustjacket.
Each copy is hand-numbered and signed by the author.

The *softcover trade edition* is covered with ten-point stock,
printed in four colors, and coated with a ultra-gloss finish.

The text of both editions is from the Adobe Garamond Family
and Engravers' Ornaments from Letterhead Fonts.
Display type is Lydian by Bitstream.

The book is printed on sixty-pound white Kateroo,
an acid-free paper, by Sheridan.